BUILDING WITH
ENGINEERED LUMBER

BUILDING WITH
ENGINEERED LUMBER

JOHN SPIER

The Taunton Press

The Taunton Press
Inspiration for hands-on living®

The Taunton Press, Inc., 63 South Main Street, PO Box 5506, Newtown, CT 06470-5506
e-mail: tp@taunton.com

Editor: Steve Cory
Interior design: Jeff Potter/Potter Publishing Studio
Layout: Laura Lind Design
Illustrator: Chuck Lockhart
Photographer: John Fournier

For Pros/By Pros® is a trademark of The Taunton Press, Inc., registered in the U.S. Patent and Trademark Office.

Library of Congress Cataloging-in-Publication Data

Spier, John.
   Building with engineered lumber / John Spier.
       p. cm. -- (For pros, by pros)
   ISBN-13: 978-1-56158-697-4
   ISBN-10: 1-56158-697-8
   1. Building, Wooden. 2. Wooden-frame buildings--Materials. 3. Engineered wood. I. Title. II. Series.
   TH1101.S675 2006
   694--dc22

                    2005030141

Printed in the United States of America
10 9 8 7 6 5 4 3 2 1

The following manufacturers/names appearing in *Building with Engineered Lumber* are trademarks: AdvanTech®, Aspenite®, Boise Cascade®, Frameworks®, Hilti®, Georgia-Pacific® Company, Google™, Louisana-Pacific®, Parallam®, Paslode®, Remington™, Sharpie®, Simpson Strong-Tie®, Stanley® Bostich, Swanson Speed Line Tools®, TimberStrand®, TrusJoist®, Weyerhaeuser®, Wolmanized®.

About Your Safety: Building is inherently dangerous. We try to promote safe work practices throughout this book, but what is safe for one builder or homeowner under certain circumstances may not be safe for you under different circumstances. So don't try anything you learn about here (or elsewhere) unless you're certain that it's safe for you. If something doesn't feel right, don't do it. Look for another way. Please keep safety foremost in your mind whenever you're working.

To Kerri, my companion, lover, best friend, and partner in everything I do…

ACKNOWLEDGMENTS

My father taught me and allowed me to use tools from an early age, and he also taught me that even in a family of academics, there is nothing unworthy about making a living with one's hands. I hope he knows somehow that I've finally written a book, too.

I've known a lot of expert carpenters over the years, some whom I've worked with, some through their writing, and some only by studying their work. I've come to realize that the best carpenters are equal parts artist, engineer, and laborer. They've set standards to which I still aspire.

My friends at The Taunton Press, most especially Roe Osborn, have taught me that building with words is as much

an art and science as building with wood. I admire their craft and appreciate their help.

Some specific thanks are due the people who worked with me during the making of this book. Thanks to Kerri and our crew, Nat Gaffett, Kate McConville, Steve Sisson, Jay Hutnak, and Marshal Bragdon; Kate and Jordan Ryan, whose new home is featured in most of the photographs; and John Fournier, who took most of the photographs. Lastly, thanks to Steve Cory, who edited my text; Chuck Lockhart, who translated my sketches into artwork; Steve Culpepper, who helped guide me in the process; and Katie Benoit, who pulled it all together and gave me my final punch lists.

Contents

Introduction   2

1 What Is Engineered Lumber?   4
A Short History of Engineered Lumber   5
Why Use Engineered Lumber?   6
Who's Using EL?   7
The Future   7

2 Types of Engineered Lumber   8
Beams, Girders, Joists, and Columns   11
Characteristics of Dimensional Lumber and EL   11
Beams and Columns   11
I-Joists   15
Trusses   16
Sheet Goods   16

3 Hardware Holds It All Together   18
The World of Steel Connectors   19
Hardware for Carrying Beams and Girders   20
Hangers of All Kinds   21
Hangers for Roof Construction   25
Tensile Connectors   27

4 Design and Planning for EL Construction   32
Fundamental Differences   33
Designing for EL   39
Hybridization   40

5 Working with Engineered Lumber   42
Safety First   42
Transportation, Care, and Handling of Engineered Lumber   45
Tools of the Trade   49
Techniques of the Trade   52
Site-Built Jigs   55

6 Beams and Girders — 56

Types of Carrying Beams — 57

Supporting the Beam — 60

Assembling and Installing Beams — 64

Finishing the Installation — 69

7 Floors—Faster and Flatter — 70

Designing the System — 70

Supporting the Floor — 73

Building the Floor — 73

8 Engineered Components in Wall Framing — 82

LSL or TimberStrand — 82

Finger-Jointed Studs — 84

Wall Headers — 85

Columns in Walls — 87

OSB Wall Sheathing — 88

9 Framing Roofs — 90

Engineered Roof Design — 91

Roofs You Can't or Shouldn't Build with EL — 94

Assembling the Engineered Roof — 94

Cover It Up! — 105

10 Trusses — 106

Types of Trusses — 107

Disadvantages of Trusses — 108

Applications for Parallel Chord Trusses — 109

Roof Trusses — 110

11 Subcontractors and the Engineered Structure — 112

Educating the Subs — 113

Utility Systems — 113

Other Subcontracting Issues — 116

Index — 120

Introduction

I started using engineered wood extensively about a decade ago. After I had designed and built a custom home in a small neighborhood, the couple who bought the lot across the street asked me to build them one just like it. I did, but because the house had already sold itself and because I had complete control over the design, engineering, and construction details, I used the house as a test platform for engineered floor systems. Today, those two houses stand side by side. They're both good houses, but I think the one built with engineered lumber is straighter and stronger than the other.

A wise engineer once referred to wood as "Miracle Fiber W." That's because, despite all of our science and technology, we've never created a material that does so many things as well as wood. What we have learned to do, from the Stone Age to the present, is to use wood better and more efficiently. This book is about engineered lumber, which is the state of the art of our use of wood today.

Since we moved out of caves, most of us have lived in homes made primarily of wood. As we've become more technologically sophisticated, our construction methods have evolved, from the primitive to today's refined framing techniques. The engineered beams, joists, columns, and rafters that are the primary focus of this book are simply the logical continuation of this process.

My own involvement in wood framing evolved almost 30 years of working in residential construction. I started out working for a remodeling company, moved into production framing, and then worked for custom homebuilders. For nearly two decades I've been a general contractor, building two to three custom homes each year, along with an equal volume of renovation and light commercial construction.

Like most of us in the building trades, I am slow to try new materials and techniques, letting others do the pioneering. However, it's obvious to me that engineered materials are the future, for many reasons. They are lighter, straighter, stronger, and more stable. They use less material, preserving resources. In many cases, they save time, too. Most important of all, though, they build a better house.

After I made the switch to engineered floor systems, I began to incorporate more engineered products into my work. Today I use engineered beams, roofs, walls, and headers as well. My wife and partner maintains that most customers are oblivious to anything but the bottom line, but we leave the jobs knowing that they got a better result. And I must say that floor squeaks and nail pops have all but disappeared from our callback lists. I like to think that in the past 10 years or so, I've climbed the steepest part of the learning curve in using engineered materials.

My goal in this book is to demystify the process of framing with engineered lumber and to share what I've learned about using it efficiently to produce high-quality results. I've tried to avoid technical jargon and to present information in useful, everyday language. At the same time, you'll find that the book equips you to speak comfortably with engineers, architects, and your lumber suppliers. I've also tried to make it an effective how-to book, so that you can order a pile of these new materials, frame a house with them, and not lose your shirt in the process. Happy hammering!

CHAPTER 1

What Is Engineered Lumber?

THE WAY WE HAVE USED WOOD for building has evolved over the millennia as we have learned to cut it into smaller pieces and to assemble the pieces into more efficient configurations. The first wood structures were bark huts and log cabins, then from those humble beginnings, we progressed to timber framing. With the advent of sawmills, we developed balloon framing and finally today's platform framing. Each system used less material to make a better product than the last. Engineered lumber (EL) products are a natural continuation of this evolutionary trend.

Timber framing is strong and beautiful, but it uses a lot of material and labor.

A Short History of Engineered Lumber

Believe it or not, the first known engineered lumber product was plywood, found in ancient Egyptian tombs dating back to 3500 B.C. In modern times, plywood is still the foremost engineered lumber product, having made its commercial debut with the advent of the rotary veneer peeler just after World War II. The building boom that followed the war fueled the demand for plywood for sheathing floors, walls, and roofs. Today, plywood remains the dominant material for those applications, although other types of engineered sheet materials such as oriented strand board (OSB) are rapidly gaining market share.

Engineered materials are beginning to impact virtually all aspects of residential construction, from form work to finish work. However, this book will focus primarily on the structural materials used for framing houses; that is, the manufactured products that are replacing traditional sawn lumber.

Glued laminated beams were first developed in Europe, probably due to a shortage of large timber. They were introduced in the United States as early as 1934 and are now manufactured throughout North America. They can be made to virtually any size and shape and in grades from rough to fancy.

In 1969, the TrusJoist® company introduced the first manufactured I-joist, consisting of top and bottom flanges of sawn lumber and a plywood web. The company followed this with laminated veneer lumber (LVL) in 1970. Within a few years, other manufacturers followed suit with similar products.

Today, the Engineered Wood Association, formerly the American Plywood Association (APA), estimates that five companies produce about 80 percent

Contact Information

Engineered materials are manufactured and distributed by companies ranging from giant global corporations to small regional lumber mills. The global giants that dominate the industry have widespread name recognition and a broad range of products and services. However, some smaller organizations have established themselves within certain regions or with specialized product lines. The seven companies listed below produce most of the engineered products featured in this book. A visit to your local lumberyard or home center will identify the companies supplying builders in your area. If you wish to search further afield, a Google™ search for "engineered lumber" will produce many thousand results.

Georgia-Pacific® Company	www.gp.com
TrusJoist (a division of Weyerhaeuser®)	www.trusjoist.com
	www.weyerhaeuser.com
Boise Cascade®	www.bc.com
Louisiana-Pacific®	www.lpcorp.com
Roseburg Forest Products	www.rfpco.com
Jager Building Systems	www.jagerbuildingsystems.com
J.M. Huber Corporation	www.huber.com

There are a number of organizations that provide extensive information and publications in support of the engineered materials industry. Two of the important ones are listed here; a visit to their websites is worthwhile. Of course, as with many other Internet-based resources, the problem is an excess of information rather than a lack of it.

Canadian Wood Council	www.cwc.ca
The Engineered Wood Association	www.apawood.org

of all I-joists, with TrusJoist holding the dominant position at about 55 percent. The remaining 20 percent of the market is held by smaller regional manufacturers, who may not provide the same range of services as the big companies but whose products are often competitively priced.

TrusJoist developed parallel strand lumber (PSL) in 1984 and laminated strand lumber (LSL) in 1992. These products are marketed as Parallam® and TimberStrand®, respectively, and as of 2004 were still protected by patents.

Why Use Engineered Lumber?

Engineered materials are generally lighter, straighter, stronger, and more stable than the comparable sawn lumber components that they replace. A house built with EL will be stronger and straighter. The floors will feel more solid and won't be as prone to squeaks and sags. Interior finishes such as drywall, tile, and flooring will look better and last longer. There will be less seasonal movement, and the building envelope will stay tighter.

There are design advantages to be gained by using EL as well. Because of the greater strength of the materials, spaces and openings can be larger. Headers and beams can be smaller, and walls can be taller. Building codes are becoming more restrictive in their requirements for wind and seismic resistance; the increased strength of EL components can help to address these issues as well.

Some images have almost become cultural icons: Along with "put a tiger in your tank," put an elephant in your living room.

Time and money

Most of us are in the construction trades to make money, and we do this in part by building things quickly and efficiently. In some applications, such as most floor structures, EL packages are much faster to assemble than conventional frames. Other EL products such as manufactured headers, columns, and corners are real time-savers, too. Of course, many of these new materials are more expensive than their traditional counterparts. Whether the labor savings outweigh the material costs is a function of labor and construction efficiency, regional price differences, and the amount of hybridization in the structure. One thing is clear, however: In the future, it will be impossible to remain economically competitive as a builder without using at least some EL materials.

Another monetary benefit of EL is price stability. Conventional lumber prices are so volatile that many suppliers change their pricing on a monthly basis, if not weekly. Although manufactured wood products are not immune to these fluctuations, the cost changes are not as extreme. This predictability allows a good builder to estimate and price more accurately, protecting both himself and his customers and ultimately reducing the building cost.

Product support

I've never gotten a warranty when I bought conventional framing lumber, and the companies selling it to me aren't ready to help me with my design and engineering. EL manufacturers, on the other hand, support me with a whole range of services, including design, engineering, estimating, training, problem solving, and extended warranties. They also advertise heavily, creating name recognition for their products and for my projects. People like seeing those elephant graphics marching along their new floor framing, just like in the magazines.

Environmental benefits

It's been said that when the Pilgrims landed at Plymouth Rock, a squirrel could have gone from there to the Mississippi River without ever touching the ground. Those virgin forests are mostly gone now, and what is left is either of lesser quality or rightfully belongs to our grandchildren. We are left with an ever-decreasing supply of premium lumber for our ever-increasing needs. Engineered lumber is part of the solution to this problem.

Good engineered lumber products can be produced using second- and third-growth or plantation-grown wood, as well as scrap and recycled materials. Also, building with engineered packages produces less scrap and waste during the construction process. The Georgia-Pacific Company has calculated that a house built primarily with engineered lumber uses approximately 50 percent less raw material than a house built using conventional methods.

Market surveys have indicated that most consumers are willing to pay a premium for homes constructed with environmentally friendly techniques and materials. If the home is not only "green" but also of higher quality, it's an easy sell. The manufacturers' advertising can help you here, as well as the many certification programs that have been adopted by states and municipalities for environmentally appropriate construction.

Who's Using EL?

According to the APA, wood I-joists had about 33 percent of the residential framing market in 1997. They are soon estimated to have at least 50 percent. OSB is replacing CDX plywood as the dominant building sheathing and to a lesser extent as subflooring as well. Headers and carrying beams made from engineered materials can be found on almost every framing job today. Roof trusses, an early form of engineered lumber framing, have been commonplace for several decades. In fact, the only aspect of residential construction where EL hasn't yet made significant inroads is in custom roof framing.

Another telling statistic is from a builder survey, also conducted by the APA, that indicates that more than 80 percent of professional builders are interested in increasing their use of engineered lumber products. These builders obviously see the advantages—and the future.

The Future

Manufacturers are continually developing new and better methods and actively promoting their use. Engineers and designers are utilizing these materials and techniques, which are becoming recognized in building codes. Builders and consumers are becoming more educated about engineered lumber, thus creating an expanded market. Following the trend, retailers are promoting their use, too. Simultaneously, supplies of conventional lumber, especially in larger dimensions and higher qualities, are dwindling, while the cost is going up. As consumers become more concerned with conservation and sustainable consumption, the industry is reacting. It is clear that engineered lumber products will command an ever-increasing share of the framing market for the foreseeable future.

Types of Engineered Lumber

LVLs, LSLs, and rim joist are all being used to start this floor frame. I-joists will be installed next.

SIMPLY STATED, ENGINEERED lumber is any structural wood product in a form that can't be sawn out of a tree. All types of EL are made by assembling small pieces of wood. Candidates for assemblage include sawdust, chips, flakes, strands, plies, veneers, and solid pieces. Products thus assembled can become beams, joists, rafters, columns, arches, trusses, sheets, stringers, and any number of custom applications. Almost all EL products are dependent on adhesives, although some are assembled with steel reinforcing and some incorporate synthetic fibers. The goal is to use materials in their most efficient manner, to achieve equivalent structural results with less weight and labor than are required when using standard lumber.

Talking Like an Engineer

In my experience, most good builders have an understanding of engineering principles, either by instinct or by education. Although this book is about construction rather than engineering, introducing some basic engineering concepts and terminology will help us to think and communicate in the same language.

To an engineer, any member resisting bending forces is a *beam*, whether the carpenter calls it a beam, girder, joist, header, or strongback. Any member being compressed from its ends is a *column*, whether it's a stud, post, strut, or bracket.

Loads are the forces applied to members. They can be *dead loads*, such as flooring, roofing, and the weight of the members themselves, or *live loads*, such as people, furniture, and snow. They can be *uniform loads*, or they can be *point loads*; they can be vertical, either up or down, or lateral, which means sideways.

Section is the cross-sectional shape of a member. If it's being used as a horizontal beam, *depth* is the height from top to bottom, and *width* is the thickness from side to side. *Thickness* is used interchangeably with *width, height* is sometimes substituted for *depth*. If a beam is being used to resist lateral loads, such as wind pressure against a wall, the depth is generally measured sideways, as it resists the load, but be careful: Not every engineer designs this way. Some manufacturers' tables will specify the strengths and allowable spans of beams in both *beam* (on edge) and *plank* (laid flat) orientations.

Tensile strength is resistance to being pulled apart by pressure from the ends. An entire member, such as a collar tie, might be in tension. *Compressive* or *axial* strength is resistance to being collapsed by pressure to the ends. A column or post resists axial loading. *Shear strength,* for our simplified purposes, is resistance to being crushed. A beam is subject to shear from below, where it is supported, or from above, where a concentrated load bears on it. Shear strength also resists the forces that would move nails sideways through the material. A beam subjected to bending stress is resisting forces internally: tensile on one side and compressive on the other.

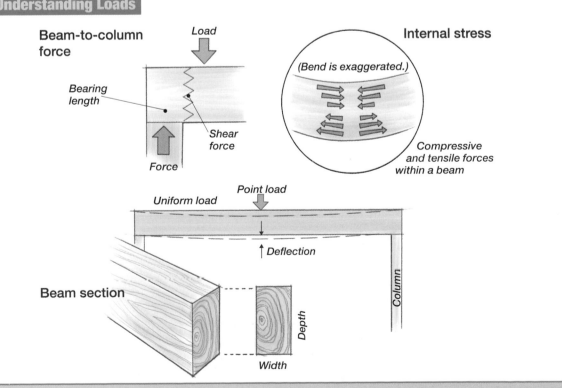

Understanding Loads

Beam-to-column force

Load

Bearing length

Shear force

Force

Internal stress

(Bend is exaggerated.)

Compressive and tensile forces within a beam

Uniform load

Point load

↑ Deflection

Beam section

Depth

Width

Column

Wood Defects

A number of possible defects often occur in sawn lumber, and some of these can also affect some types of EL. Here, I'll use the most common terms for these defects, although you may encounter others.

▪ Curves: There are three ways a piece of lumber can curve: crown, bow, and twist. Of course, a single piece of wood can have all of these conditions at once. The same terms would apply to a piece of EL: Glulams often have crown; LVLs are prone to bow and twist; and I-joists are sometimes bowed or twisted but are almost never crowned.

▪ Cupping: Cupping is caused when one side of a board is wetted or dried more than the other. It is also a natural condition caused by the grain in many pieces of sawn lumber. LVLs are susceptible to cupping if they are allowed to lie on the ground or on a wet floor.

▪ Knots: Sawn lumber has knots, unless it is an expensive "clear" grade. These can range from small tight knots (STK) in select lumber to large, loose knots that destroy the integrity of the board. With the exception of glulams, EL materials do not contain knots.

▪ Checks and splits: Sawn lumber, especially in large dimensions, is liable to contain checks and splits. Sometimes these were present in the tree before it was cut; more often, they result from rapid and uneven drying. They can render large sections of a piece of lumber unusable. Most EL is immune to checking and splitting, although repeated wetting and drying can cause it in the ends of PSL material.

▪ Bark, wane, or shake: When a piece of lumber is sawn from the edge of a tree, a portion of its rectangular shape is sometimes lost or is composed of bark. This can reduce structural values, as well as make it more difficult to work with.

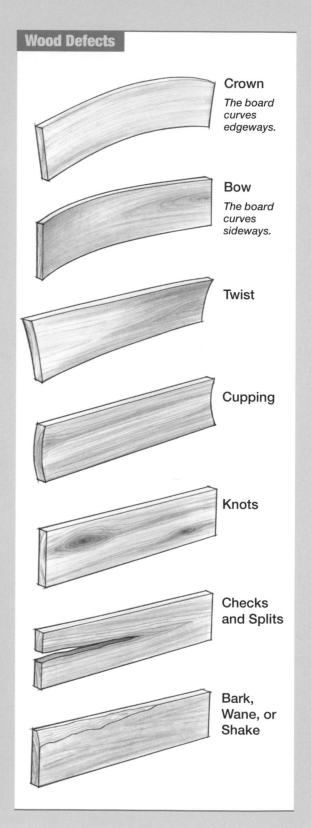

Wood Defects

Crown
The board curves edgeways.

Bow
The board curves sideways.

Twist

Cupping

Knots

Checks and Splits

Bark, Wane, or Shake

Beams, Girders, Joists, and Columns

All horizontal members—those that are supported from underneath and loaded on top—are called beams by engineers. Carpenters, however, have their own terminology. For consistency in this book, I'll refer to joists as the closely spaced and uniformly loaded members used to frame most floors and ceilings. The beams that support joists I'll call girders or carrying beams, unless they form openings, in which case I'll call them headers. Openings can be in floors, walls, ceilings, or roofs; they're all still made with headers. Members that stand upright and carry vertical loads are columns or posts. For more on terms, see the sidebar on p. 9.

The first beams and columns were logs; as building techniques progressed, they were squared into timbers. With improved cutting and engineering technology, squared beams evolved into deeper rectangular sections. Most conventional framing today uses wood in this form. Interestingly, the round column section is the most efficient structural form; making columns from square or rectangular sections just makes them more convenient to cut, transport, and use.

Characteristics of Dimensional Lumber and EL

Beams and columns made of solid wood are simple and functional but not highly efficient. They also have structural deficiencies, which are increasingly more prevalent as the world's supply of straight, clear, virgin first-growth timber dwindles and becomes more expensive.

Natural defects such as knots, checks, splits, and irregular grain direction all limit the design strength of wooden sections (see the sidebar on the facing page). In addition, sawn lumber is almost never perfectly straight; twists, bends, cups, and crowns all affect structural integrity and usability. Lastly, wood is prone to shrinkage and other movement with age and with changes in humidity and temperature.

Engineered materials address the inherent liabilities of sawn lumber in several ways. First, EL is made of homogeneous material, without defects, so that the structural characteristics are uniform, dependable, and can be maximized. Second, the material is oriented in its most efficient configuration. And third, by manufacturing products in a controlled environment and designing them for stability, EL eliminates variations in size, shape, and strength.

Beams and Columns

The choice of material for beams and columns is dictated by structural requirements and cost efficiency and sometimes by aesthetics.

Dimension lumber

A solid piece of wood is still a good choice for many applications, and most people would agree that it is also the most attractive one, although a clean and bright glulam can be beautiful, too. Engineered or manufactured alternatives have the advantages of strength, stability, and sometimes economy, so today the use of solid timber, at least in large sizes, is primarily for appearance.

Beam Types

Solid wood

Pros: Simple, inexpensive, available, aesthetic

Cons: Inefficient, unstable

Glulam

Pros: Stronger than wood, available in shapes and grades, aesthetically pleasing

Cons: Heavy, must be special-ordered, expensive

Parallel strand lumber

Pros: Very strong, available in large sizes, available pressure treated

Cons: Heavy, not pleasing to most eyes

Laminated strand lumber

Pros: Moderately strong, available in standard framing sizes, softer than PSL or LVL

Cons: Sensitive to moisture

Laminated veneer lumber

Pros: Standard thickness, ideal for built-up assemblies, strong, often available in stock, versatile

Cons: Less stable than PSL or LSL, slippery and dangerous to work with

LSL (laminated strand lumber)

Solid wood

PSL (parallel strand lumber)

LVL (laminated veneer lumber)

Glu-lam

Glulams

Laminated beams, often called glulams, have been available for many years. They are manufactured in long lengths in a variety of sizes, most commonly of southern yellow pine. The splices are finger-jointed and staggered, then the entire assembly is glued, pressed, and sanded. The beams are available in grades from "rough construction" to "clean & bright." They can be custom built to almost any size, length, and shape; they can even be curved. The beams are about 25 percent stronger than comparable solid timber, depending on species and grade, and they are much more stable; they don't shrink, twist, check, or split. Traditional uses include exposed carrying beams and roof ridges, as well as hybrid timber frame structures with long, clear spans.

Parallel strand lumber (PSL)

Parallel strand lumber is made by gluing or bonding long strands of wood together to make large beam or column sections. TrusJoist holds the patent on these beams, marketing them under the name Parallam. The company makes beams 1¾ in. to 7 in. wide and 9¼ in. to 18 in. deep, and columns from 3½ in. square to 7 in. square. PSL is the strongest and stiffest wood section available. For large beams that can be set in position in one piece, it's often the most effective choice. PSL is also available Wolmanized®, or pressure treated, making it the best choice for exterior or other potentially wet applications.

Architectural-grade glulams make a beautiful ridge and rafters in this home.

The exposed beam carrying this second-floor deck is made from treated PSL material.

This short LSL is being prepped to become a flush beam over a hallway.

Two built-up LVL beams are ready to carry the first floor of this house.

Laminated strand lumber (LSL)

Laminated strand lumber is another Trus-Joist proprietary patented product, which it markets under the name TimberStrand. It is similar to PSL except that the strands are shorter and are not necessarily as parallel. The resulting product is not as strong as PSL, but it is much less expensive. For beams, LSL is available in 1¾-in. and 3½-in. widths, in depths from 7¼ in. to 18 in. Columns are available in sizes comparable to those available in PSL.

LSL is the material most often used for rim joist stock, wall-framing material, and specialized shapes such as 45-degree wall-corner columns. LSL is not available treated and in fact is susceptible to swelling and delamination in wet conditions. Because LSL is reasonably strong, stable, soft, easily worked, and relatively inexpensive, it is the standard choice for many beams, rafters, and headers. LSL also has good shear strength, making it a suitable choice for beams and headers where the available bearing length is limited.

Laminated veneer lumber (LSL)

Laminated veneer lumber is manufactured by bonding plies together into a rectangular beam section. This results in a section that is strong in its vertical dimension—that is, when used upright. LVLs are made in a standard 1¾-in. thickness and in depths from 5¼ in. to 18 in. The 1¾-in. thickness is generally used in built-up members of two, three, or four plies.

A beam built up from multiple LVLs is almost as strong as a PSL beam of the same size, with the advantages that it can be assembled in place by a smaller crew and can be spliced into longer lengths than can be easily handled as single members. LVL is a versatile material: It can be ripped to custom sizes, shapes, and bevels; it makes a fine stair stringer; and with its excellent holding power, it is a good substitute for rim-joist material where ledgers need to be attached.

There are some drawbacks to LVL. It is prone to cupping, which makes it difficult to assemble into beams of consistent thickness and also makes cutting a challenge at times. There are some safety issues as well; refer to p. 44 for more information.

I-Joists

I-joists are the standard material in EL floor and roof framing, taking the place of standard 2x10s or 2x12s. Like a steel I-beam, they get their strength by moving material to where it is the most efficient. The flanges take the tensile, compressive, and lateral loads; the web is primarily a spacer that keeps the flanges in position. Shear loads and concentrated compressive loads on I-joists often require reinforcement of the webs. This is done with blocks of material called web stiffeners, which transfer these loads from one flange to the other.

I-joists differ in flange and web material, as well as in size, shape, and strength. The flanges can be solid lumber or EL, either LSL, LVL, or PSL. The web material is typically OSB but sometimes is plywood. Flange widths range from 1¾ in. to 3½ in. and depths from 9½ in. to 20 in. (The available depths are intentionally different from that of standard nominal sawn lumber to keep them from being mixed.)

I-joist flanges can be made of almost any material, and in fact, I've gotten framing deliveries that had more than one type of flange in the same floor package. I much prefer the LSL flanges; they

I-Joists

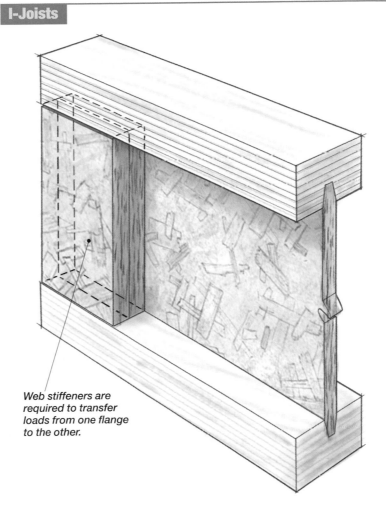

Web stiffeners are required to transfer loads from one flange to the other.

An I-joist gets its strength by using a stronger material at the top and bottom edges where the tensile and compressive loads are concentrated. The web primarily holds the flanges in position, which is why it can be drilled extensively.

This is a standard I-joist with a web stiffeners installed. Note that the stiffener fits tightly on the bottom flange but leaves +/-⅛ in. at the top flange.

> ■ **PRO TIP**
>
> I-joists are delicate and moisture sensitive. They need to be stored and handled carefully and kept as dry as possible. A floor or roof made with bad I-joists is a bad floor or roof, period.

Standardization of I-Joists

Looking at the vast array of sizes, shapes, types, and design properties of I-joists, you are bound to wonder: Why aren't there industry standards? Standardization is high on the wish list of many building officials and code writers. There is no easy answer; it's an industry goal but controversial. There are conflicting agendas, including the protection of market share, proprietary technology, and cost. Look for standardization someday but probably not soon.

Meanwhile, given that most I-joists are utilized in preengineered packages, this is not a big problem for builders. It might be an issue if you wanted to substitute leftover materials from one job to another. Armed with the span and load tables from both manufacturers, you should be able to check for interchangeability, but clear it with your building inspector first.

are the most durable and the least likely to split when they are nailed. In my opinion, the solid lumber flanges are the worst option; they can split, squeak, and separate from the webs when they get wet. I've read articles that tell me other framers may feel exactly the opposite, though, so try them out and decide for yourself.

Some I-joists come with premarked or punched knockouts for plumbing and wiring. For these to be useful, the I-joists need to be aligned and installed so that the factory-cut ends run consistently along one edge of the floor. My experience has been that high-quality subcontractors prefer to drill their own neat rows of holes, while other subs just knock out whichever holes are convenient with a hammer.

Trusses

Both bar (floor) and roof trusses qualify as engineered lumber, since they are both "assemblies of wood components." The use of trusses is an involved subject that would warrant an entire book of its own. Because they are engineered components, I'll address them in chapter 10, but it will by no means be a comprehensive treatment.

The hybrid bar truss/I-joist is an intriguing product that I've seen advertised but hasn't yet become generally available. This is a joist built as a bar truss with wood flanges and a steel web but with several feet on each end built as a conventional I-joist. These have the strength and utility advantages of the bar truss but can be easily trimmed to length, thus eliminating the major disadvantage of the bar truss.

Sheet Goods

Plywood is the original engineered lumber product, having replaced solid-wood sheathing back in the 1950s when it became readily available. Regular plywood, with perpendicularly glued layers of peeled wood veneer, is still the predominant sheet material used in residential construction. However, in recent decades, several other types of sheet goods have made significant inroads.

OSB is made of oriented, pressed, and glued strands. Available primarily in $\frac{7}{16}$-in. thickness, this material replaces $\frac{1}{2}$-in. CDX plywood and is of similar strength. In EL framing, it is also used to make web stiffeners. OSB has some advantages as wall and roof sheathing: It is less expensive than plywood, and it has lines marked on it that assist in measuring, layout, and nailing. It is not subject to voids and delamination, like plywood. However, the edges tend to swell up in moist conditions.

Flakeboard, or Aspenite®, is OSB without the orientation, quality control, or strength rating. It has little application in structural framing.

AdvanTech® subflooring, manufactured by Huber Engineered Woods, LLC, is a replacement for standard tongue-and-groove underlayment-grade plywood. (There are similar products made by other manufacturers, but this is the one I am familiar with.) Available in ¾-in. and 1⅛-in. thicknesses, this material is stable, strong, and less expensive than plywood. Like OSB, however, it is less durable in wet conditions.

Here are some I-joists in assorted sizes, made with LVL flanges and OSB woods.

CHAPTER 3

Hardware Holds It All Together

E ARLY IN HUMAN HISTORY, men realized that wood is a nearly ideal blend of compressive and tensile strength and that its primary structural limitation was in fastening pieces of it together. Structures like log cabins relied either on gravity and pure compression or on lashings with tensile materials such as ropes and vines. In fact, some of the most sophisticated examples of old engineering are lashed structures, such as suspension bridges and Polynesian outrigger canoes; even early airplanes were made of wood, cable, and canvas.

Complex structures rely on a blend of compressive and tensile elements, each used in their most appropriate and efficient locations. Wooden elements are efficient in both tension and compression; however, wood is limited when it comes to shear strength—the connections between pieces. This problem was first addressed by using tightly engineered joints and pegs in timber-frame construction. As construction progressed to platform framing with smaller sawn lumber members, the attachment system regressed to almost pure compression; the few tensile connections in a platform structure are nailed and have limited strength. With the advent of engineered lumber materials, strong fastening again became important, so steel connectors have evolved to fill this need.

Incidentally, the next generation of wood structures will probably be glued and laminated together, with the fibers oriented exactly along the load paths and with shapes that are designed to be self-supporting. This approach is already widespread in boat building but so far has seen only limited application in other wooden structures.

The World of Steel Connectors

Steel-framing connectors—ranging from simple plates to joist hangers and column bases to complex specialty items—have been with us for a long time. However, it is only recently, with the advent of new materials, techniques, and building codes, that connectors have really come into their own as an integral part of most wood structures.

Because the function of most steel connectors is to "hang" one member from another, we refer to many of these items as "hangers." Other connectors are referred to generically as ties, straps, hold-downs, or simply as connectors.

Fasteners for steel connectors

Manufacturers specify the number and size of nails required for each connector. In many cases, there are more holes in the hardware than the specified number of nails. If the utmost in efficiency is important to you, nail according to spec; otherwise, fill all the holes. Most nails

should be installed using a pneumatic nailer, which will shoot hardened galvanized nails 1½ in. or 2½ in. long. I've heard stories of building officials asking for nails to be pulled to verify that the correct ones were used; fixing an error in this department would be a nightmare, so have both types of nails on hand and do it right. You should also keep a supply of regular hanger nails for hand nailing. Many hangers can be fastened with regular framing nails, and some require them. Hot-dipped galvanized nails are nice for their pull-out resistance, but this virtue makes it difficult to pull them out if you make a mistake. The difference between regular framing nails and hanger nails (sometimes called Teco nails) is in shear strength, which is a function of diameter and hardening. If hanger nails are specified, use them.

Simpson Strong-Tie®

The Simpson Strong-Tie Company (SST) has become so dominant in the residential framing connector industry that its products and applications almost define the

Hanger nails of two lengths, such as these, are typically used on most jobs. The nails shown are for the Paslode® Positive Placement Nailer and are 1½ in. and 2½ in. long. They are hardened and galvanized. The longer nails are identified by color for the benefit of the engineer or building inspector, who may need to verify that the correct nails were used in a given installation.

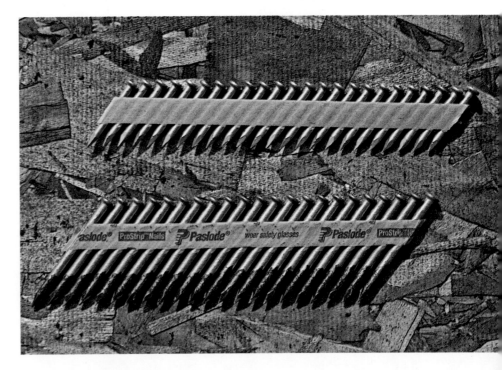

■ **PRO TIP**

I recently got the most current copy of the Simpson catalog and found that new products were listed in red ink in the index. Looking them up, I found that the company had solved some problems I'd long wondered about. It's worth ordering a new catalog every year, instead of relying on a tattered old friend.

codes. Most sets of specifications reference its products, and other manufacturers often identify their own products with "Simpson equivalent" designations. You can contact the company, either directly or through your local supplier, to obtain a Simpson catalog or even an entire set of catalogs and specification books. These are well worth reading through and becoming familiar with. Often a working knowledge of available products will help in designing a structural system for a custom or non-standard application. Also, most building officials will accept alternate techniques if you can back up your argument with the appropriate tables and charts.

Types of steel connectors

There are two basic categories of job-site-installed connectors: those that are used in the actual assembly of the structure and those that are added to the structure after it is assembled to strengthen it and to meet code requirements. Buildings using engineered lumber are heavily dependent on both types. A dissertation on all of the connectors available would require a book of its own (the Simpson catalog is pretty close); here, I'll provide an overview of the types of connectors you'll most often use with engineered lumber, along with tips on choosing and using them.

Hardware for Carrying Beams and Girders

The only hardware item specific to engineered lumber carrying beams is the Lally column cap, which is now required by most building codes. These are designated with a number that gives the width of the beam and the diameter of the column. For instance, an LCC5.25-3.5 accommodates three LVLs with a total width of 5¼ in. and rests on top of a 3½-in. column. (Lally column caps are a bit tricky to install; see p. 63 for installation tips.)

Sometimes a hardware attachment will be specified where an EL beam rests on a wood or EL column. There is a Simpson connector for virtually any situation like this; just look in the catalog. There are even specialty connectors that can be cast in place to attach beams to concrete.

Occasionally, a set of plans will call for girders or carrying beams that intersect in the same plane, usually in the shape of a T. The loads on these members preclude using any type of stock connector, so there are two approaches to solving the problem. The best is to support them independently, using separate

These are some of the catalogs available from Simpson Strong-Tie. They are often supplied as a complete package in a three-ring binder.

These Lally column caps are a code requirement in many jurisdictions today. They are difficult to retrofit, so if you need them, get them before you start.

columns. If this is not feasible, a custom-built hanger using steel angle iron and machine bolts can be used. Either way, the connections should be checked and approved by an engineer.

When setting beams and girders, it helps to have on hand a collection of steel bearing plates. I keep a box of scrap steel plate in various thicknesses on site. This stock can be cut into pieces and used as shims to adjust the height of beams resting in beam pockets or on columns; it also can be used under Lally columns when they get cut too short.

Hangers of All Kinds

Joist and beam hangers are familiar items; they've been used in conventional framing for years. Engineered lumber systems are even more dependent on these hangers. The concepts remain the same, but there is a dizzying array of choices

When Two Carrying Beams Intersect

Two girders connected with a steel hanger of welded angle iron

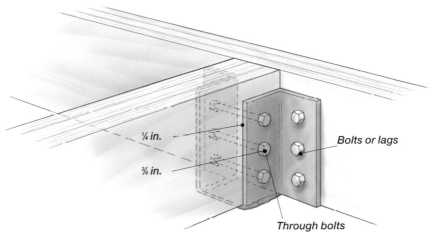

¼ in.

¾ in.

Bolts or lags

Through bolts

An engineer's approval is required for all such connections.

This connection can be made with two opposing pieces of angle iron, omitting the bottom plate and welding, provided through-bolt connections are used.

Using two columns to carry two beams

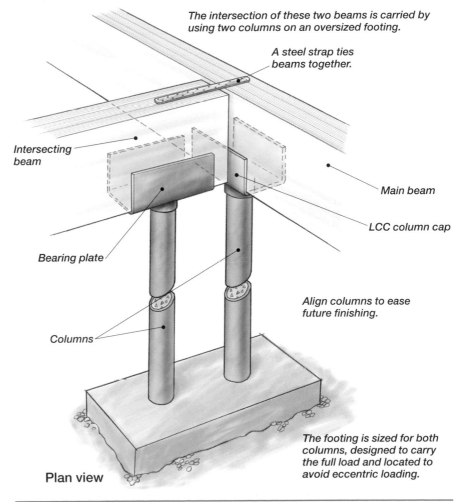

The intersection of these two beams is carried by using two columns on an oversized footing.

A steel strap ties beams together.

Intersecting beam

Main beam

LCC column cap

Bearing plate

Align columns to ease future finishing.

Columns

The footing is sized for both columns, designed to carry the full load and located to avoid eccentric loading.

Plan view

Steel Bearing Plates

Assorted thicknesses of ⅛ in., ¼ in., and ⅜ in.

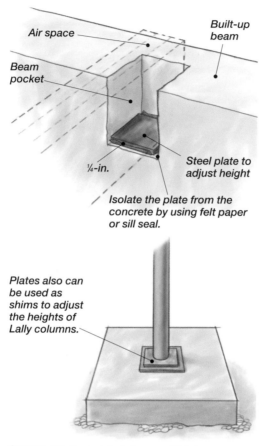

Air space

Built-up beam

Beam pocket

¼-in.

Steel plate to adjust height

Isolate the plate from the concrete by using felt paper or sill seal.

Plates also can be used as shims to adjust the heights of Lally columns.

Steel plates in assorted sizes and thicknesses can be used as shims to adjust heights and to provide flat bearing surfaces.

and applications. Don't panic—usually the engineer or manufacturer will select them for you, based on the materials being connected and the anticipated loads. There are often several options, so as you become familiar with them, you'll develop personal preferences.

There are several ways in which hangers are classified. The first is by the members being installed in them. There are specific hangers for every size I-joist, LVL, and other beam and for doubles, triples, and quadruples of these members. The next classification is according to the way in which they are attached. Most hangers are either face-nailed or top-

flanged, but some are nailed through concealed flanges, some are bolted or lagged, and some are welded. Finally, all hangers are classified according to allowable load. Lighter-gauge hangers are used to support simple rafters and joists, and progressively heavier and more expensive hangers are specified for bigger loads. Some hangers are rated for uplift loads for wind resistance or cantilevered applications; some are not. Additionally, all hangers have a fastening schedule that gives the number and size of nails or bolts needed to support a given load. Lastly, there are specialty hangers; those that can be skewed left, right, up, down, or both and those that need to be specially ordered for specific applications.

Like most builders, I tend to err on the side of ordering extra bits and pieces of hardware, which I then save forever. I now have several large boxes of miscellaneous hardware, some of which I can't even identify. But every once in a while that stuff rescues me from some impossible dilemma.

I-joist hangers

I-joists require special hangers because only the top and bottom flanges can be side-nailed. In regular, light-duty applications where an I-joist is attached to a beam, a typical installation would use an IUT face-nailed tabbed hanger. This hanger is face-nailed to the supporting beam, the joist is dropped in, and the small nailing tabs are bent down and nailed to the bottom flange.

The other type of hanger commonly used for I-joists is a top-mounted, or flanged, hanger. In a light-duty application, this might be an SST ITT. This hanger will support loads in a simple floor assembly and is similar to the IUT hanger. The ITT differs from an IUT in that it has a top flange that is nailed on top of the supporting member. The most

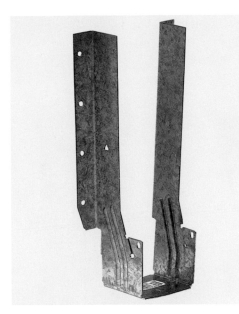

The IUT is a standard light-duty hanger for attaching I-joists to flush beams or ledgers. It is strictly face-nailed and has tabs that bend down to hold the bottom joist flange.

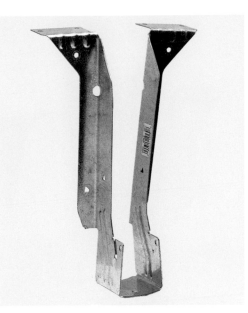

The ITT is the standard light-duty top flange hanger for I-joists. It resembles the IUT, but is attached to the beam or ledger only through its top flange.

frequent application for these is installation on top of a steel I-beam, either on a plate bolted to the top of the beam or welded on directly. Either way, the top flange is a mixed blessing. It is fast to install and guarantees a consistent height, but the height is not adjustable, and the flanges can make a bump under the subfloor.

As the required strength increases for I-joist hangers, there is an array of larger and heavier hangers available. These can include HIT-, MIT-, LBV-, and W-type hangers. These hangers are either top-flange mounted, face-nailed, or both and require additional fasteners. They often need web stiffeners to be installed, as well.

Heavy-duty hangers

Carrying beams or headers can be made of LVL, LSL, or PSL stock in various dimensions. Your plot plan will identify hangers for these members based on size, fastening requirements, and load. If you substitute other hangers, use the manu-

facturer's tables to make sure that those you are using are equivalently strong.

These heavy-duty hangers install much like I-joist hangers, but the beams they support are often much bigger and

I-Joist Hanger Installation

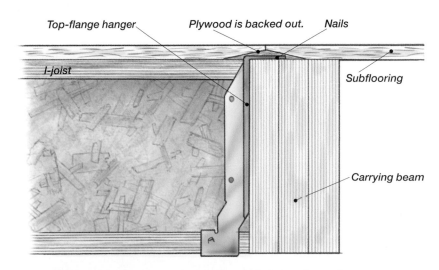

Backing out the subflooring to clear the hanger flanges is fast and easy; I use my circular saw with the blade guard held back. There are slower and safer methods if you're not comfortable doing that.

These four photos show an assortment of top-flanged hangers available from SST. They are selected or specified according to requirements for strength and attachment method.

Heavy-Duty Flange Hanger

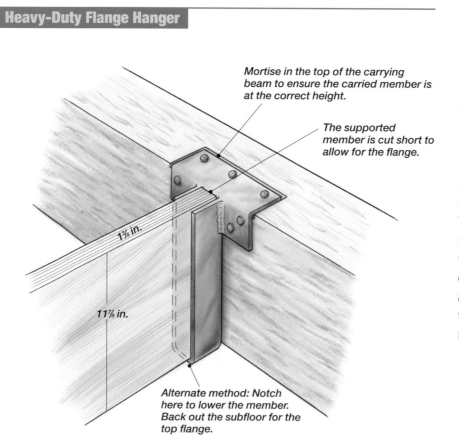

Mortise in the top of the carrying beam to ensure the carried member is at the correct height.

The supported member is cut short to allow for the flange.

1¾ in.

11⅞ in.

Alternate method: Notch here to lower the member. Back out the subfloor for the top flange.

The flanges of these hangers are thick enough so that some method must be employed to ensure that the two beams are the same height.

hard to handle. Having one drop or slip with a bunch of sharp jagged hardware on it can be lethal. It is usually safest to install the hanger first, and then slip the beam into the hanger. But sometimes it's much faster to preinstall the hangers on the beam before setting it in place.

Some of the heavier-duty hangers have significant flange thicknesses and may require some finesse to install and finish properly. For instance, many of the W-series hangers have top flanges ¼ in. or more in thickness. These must be mortised into the carrying member, both to clear the surface plane for the subflooring and to get the two members aligned vertically. Some flanges also require adjustment of the beam length to fit properly.

Hangers for Roof Construction

Roof construction with EL involves many of the same issues as with floor framing but also has the complications introduced by slope. These include pitched and skewed connections and mixed material depths. Roofs sometimes use specially made hangers; because this type of construction is newly evolving, it often requires creative adaptations.

Rafter hangers

The mainstay of EL roof construction is the I-joist rafter, and the workhorse connector for these is a hanger that can be sloped or skewed, such as the SST LSSUI. These versatile hangers are stock items that will handle all of the routine connections between rafters, jack rafters, ridges, hips, and valleys. (For installation instructions, see p. 31. These hangers require web stiffeners and careful nailing, and the manufacturer cautions that they should only be bent one time.)

Hangers for headers in roofs

Top-flange I-joist hangers are clearly unsuited for roof construction, but most of the face-mounted hangers can be specified and used for supporting headers and ridges within roofs. Usually, these are simple applications, where the hangers are nailed on the side of a structural rafter and the supported member dropped into them. Often, a plumb header in a roof will require that one side of the hanger be cut shorter or bent over and nailed on top of the rafter. Since the header being used is generally oversized for the roof thickness, this shouldn't be a problem.

Shim Before Cutting Subfloor

Openings in floors are often framed with top-flanged hangers. If you subfloor over these openings and then cut them out, it's easy to saw through the top flange of the hanger, thus destroying its structural integrity. Use a wooden wedge or a flatbar to keep your sawblade off of the hanger.

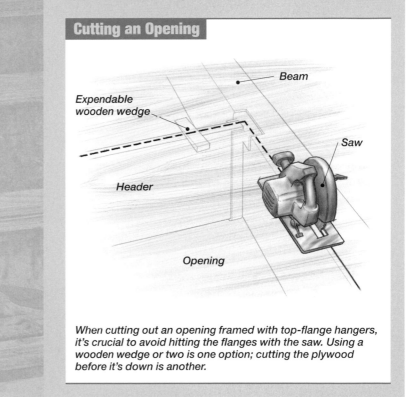

Cutting an Opening

Beam

Expendable wooden wedge

Saw

Header

Opening

When cutting out an opening framed with top-flange hangers, it's crucial to avoid hitting the flanges with the saw. Using a wooden wedge or two is one option; cutting the plywood before it's down is another.

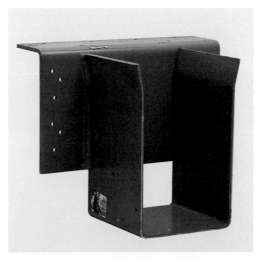

The SST LSSUI rafter hanger is adjustable, to handle a variety of situations.

▪ PRO TIP

Like any other engineered system, a hanger is only as strong as its weakest link. If you cut off half of one side flange, you might think you've only reduced its strength by one quarter, but you've actually reduced it by half. If in doubt, use a stronger hanger or pick one that can be wrapped over the top of the rafter for an even stronger connection.

These two hangers were custom-made to carry doubled LVL rafters against a ridge.

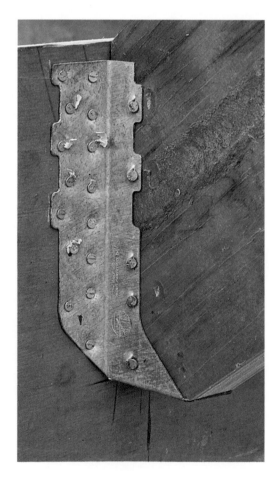

Rather than order a custom hanger with an upward slope, the worker adapted the rafter to fit a stock HGUS hanger.

Custom-made hangers

In a complex roof system and occasionally in a floor system, the plot plan will specify hangers that need to be custom-made. Their size, pitch, and skew are specifically designated. As you might expect, they are expensive and take a while to get, but if you review the plan carefully ahead of time, this is not a problem. Having the correct hardware pays for itself in time savings.

Hangers "not found"

A manufacturer will sometimes provide a plot plan, again usually for a roof but occasionally for a floor, which specifies a hanger in a location on the plan but lists it in the hardware schedule as "not found." If this happens to you, first look through the catalog to see if there is a connector that will work. Next, call your supplier, get the person who did the specifications on the line, and discuss the options. Often, a creative solution can be arrived at by using an alternative connector or some combination of plates and straps. If all else fails, you'll need to have a piece of hardware custom-made.

Hip, ridge, and valley connectors

In recent years, engineers have decided that hips, ridges, and valleys are structural members and have designed their load calculations accordingly. Not only has this resulted in much larger members but also has created a need for large, specialized hangers at the ends. Examples of these are SST HCPs (hip corner plates) and SST HRCs (hip ridge connectors). The key to using these connectors is to carefully examine the drawing ahead of time so you can organize the assembly sequence.

HCP hangers can only be installed after the hip rafter is in place if there is no bird's-mouth cut. The catalog drawing shows it this way, but in reality most hip rafters are deeper than the rafters they carry and thus need to be notched down to the rafter plane.

HRC connectors, which carry two opposing hip or valley rafters against a ridge or header, also need to be preinstalled. This is counterintuitive for many of us who have developed our techniques while installing conventional framing. For instance, where two hips meet the end of a ridge, most of us install the ridge and common rafters before addressing the hips. If you do this, the HRC can't be installed. Similarly, where two valley rafters meet a dormer header or intersecting ridge, most of us install the ridge first, then the valleys. Again, if you do this, the HRC can't be installed.

Variable-pitch rafter connections

Most of the time, I-joists used as rafters are cut with bird's mouths, as in conventional framing. However, another technique, which may find its way into common usage in production framing, is the use of variable-pitch seat connections. These require adjustment of the building section and may complicate eaves and trim, but they are fast and strong. Just nail the connectors to the plates, drop the rafters in, and nail the flanges.

Tensile Connectors

The remainder of the hardware typically used in EL construction is installed after assembly, although in some cases prior to sheathing. These connectors add tensile strength to joints between members and create the load paths that resist uplift and tie the entire structure to the foundation. There is little here that differs from conventional framing with today's building

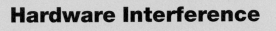

Hardware Interference

Often, a plan will include framing members attached with hardware in close proximity so that one piece of hardware interferes with attaching the next. A typical example is an I-joist next to a header, where the two hangers' flanges would overlap. The easiest way to fix this on-site is to shift the layout, but sometimes this introduces other problems. A better fix is to anticipate the issue by careful study of the plan and to combine the members into a single larger hanger. Be sure to check the cumulative strength of both the combined members and the new hardware.

Hardware and the New Treated Lumber

As this book is being written, the familiar CCA-treated lumber is being phased out. Although more environmentally friendly, the new replacement formulas for treated wood have the potential to react with conventional framing hardware. Simpson Strong-Tie recommends using hardware with its heavier galvanizing treatments for these applications, but the issue is in flux. Consult your supplier and building official for current requirements.

The HCP, or hip corner plate, connects a rafter or joist to double top plates at a 45 degree angle.

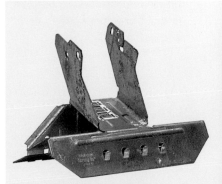

The VPR, or variable-pitch rafter connector, allows the attachment of rafters to a top plate without cutting a bird's mouth. This facilitates using I-joist rafters in situations where the flanges can't be notched or cut, such as at intermediate or nonbearing walls.

Installing HD connectors like these requires careful attention to anchor-bolt placement, framing layout, and construction sequence. It's easy to get into a situation where they are difficult or impossible to drill and bolt in.

codes, so I'll just touch on the hardware specific to EL structures.

Wall connections

Walls that incorporate structural EL columns often use those columns to resist tensile or uplift loads, as well as to support weight. Because of the greater forces involved, these columns are usually specified with large bolt-on connections to the foundation, beams, upper floors, or roofs. Key to installing these connections is careful planning; study the connector in the catalog and visualize the attachment sequence.

Rafter connections

As in conventional framing, rafters are required to have tensile connectors at both ends. In some cases, the specified hanger serves this function; in other cases, an additional piece of hardware is required.

These ridge straps were specified as LSTA 36, but they were cut using compound snips from a coil of equivalent stock for a considerable savings.

The roof on this small addition was secured against uplift by using H2.5 rafter ties.

RT-20 rafter ties secure these rafters to both the stud and the top plates.

Ridge ties are often specified over the tops of rafters and ridges, particularly in what are considered "steep slope applications" (at least 4/12). Typically, the plot plan will specify an SST strap tie, such as an LSTA. The catalog will show details such as length, width, gauge, and fastener size and pattern. Using this information, the straps can be cut from bulk coiled strap material for a considerable savings and increased versatility. Key to efficiency here is having the rafters oppose each other across the ridge; if they don't, each rafter can be strapped independently to the ridge.

An alternate ridge connector that I like to use is a non-Simpson product, United Steel Products (USP) RT-20. This handy connector, in addition to being a good rafter tie, is a good way to tie opposing rafters together across a ridge. Because it nails on the side of the flanges and offsets to one side over the ridge, it

■ PRO TIP

Should straps be installed under or over the sheathing? I like to sheath over my straps for increased strength, ease of location, corrosion resistance, permanence, and as a courtesy to the roofer. However, the alternate approach, strapping over the plywood, has advantages, too. It's easier to do while standing on the plywood or staging, and you don't need to nail through the straps when sheathing.

Removing a Joist Hanger

Every once in a while, a hanger gets installed incorrectly—too high or low, on the wrong mark, or the wrong hanger for the location. Removing one is a real pain, so the first rule is that "he who made the mistake shall fix it." You will have to decide whether it is worth the trouble to save the hanger. If you have extra hangers, it's easiest to rip the thing off with a cat's paw and throw it in the dumpster. Often, though, it's your last one, and an expensive one, too, so it will be worth your while to save it.

If you can, work the flanges out evenly by driving a sharp flatbar behind the flange at each nail, wedging it out just enough to pull from the front without damaging the hanger. If the nails are really tenacious—16d hot-dipped galvies in LVL, for instance—I wedge myself just enough space to slip a reciprocating saw blade in and cut them off all at once. Otherwise, I pull the nails. Alternatively, zip the nail heads off using an angle grinder. If the beam in the hanger does not have to be kept intact, you can cut it near the hanger and split it out in little pieces. Then the nails can come out of the sides without deforming the hanger.

Two types of hangers are pretty much nonsalvageable. One is any galvanized hanger in an exterior location; pulling it ruins the protective coating. The other is a double shear nailed hanger, where the side nails are toenailed into the supporting beam.

Ways to Remove a Hanger

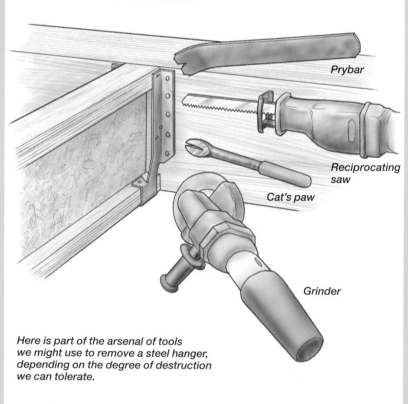

Prybar

Reciprocating saw

Cat's paw

Grinder

Here is part of the arsenal of tools we might use to remove a steel hanger, depending on the degree of destruction we can tolerate.

doesn't interfere with nailing sheathing or roofing.

The lower ends of rafters also need connectors to resist uplift forces. There is a wide range of hardware for this application. These connections are not usually specified by the EL manufacturer, since they are building-code defined. Select them based on rafter length and pitch, code requirements, and personal preference. Depending on whether I am fastening the rafter to a stud, top plate, or header, I use one of several ties.

Creative adaptation

There are situations where neither the building code nor the EL plan prescribes a piece of hardware but where common sense dictates additional security. Examples of these are post-to-ridge connections; posts between floors, beams, or headers to plates; ceiling joists that may act as tensile connections; and interior details that are not part of the engineered structure but that require structural integrity. Using a coil of strap material and a box of assorted connectors, you can make a strong and effective connection. Sometimes, the goal is nothing more than making it less likely that a future remodeler will remove a critical component, such as a post in an attic.

Many Ways to Hang a Hanger

There are several ways to install hangers; it's a matter of personal preference and what best fits the situation. Here are some methods:

▪ Attach the hangers to the beam before you put the beam in place. This is fast and easy, if you get your layout right. Set the beam on sawhorses, square your layout marks, get a box of hangers, and spike them all on. Do both sides, if you want. Just be careful lifting it, and don't swap ends.

▪ Set the beam first, then the hangers. This is safer both for layout and for lifting. Set a plank on horses or ladders at a good working height, and nail the hangers on where they go. Sometimes it's easier to nail just one side of the hanger so that the joist can be rolled into place and the hanger nailed tight. Some people nail both sides of the hanger using a cutoff as a gauge for width; I find that I can gauge them by eye just as well.

▪ Attach the hangers to the joists first. This is quick and ensures perfect height. Set the joists upside down on horses or the pile, tack the hangers on with a nail through the bottom, and use them to nail the joists in place.

▪ Set the joists in place, then install the hangers. This method works where there are a bunch of interior walls for the joists to rest on. It also ensures perfect height.

CHAPTER 4

Design and Planning for EL Construction

MOST OF WHAT WE DO when framing with EL is adaptation of familiar conventional framing methods. In fact, EL components have been working their way into conventional framing for the past several decades, so the process is very much evolutionary and hybridized. However, there are both general concepts and specific considerations we must incorporate when adapting or designing structures to be built primarily with EL. In addition, at this stage in the evolution of framing, we still need to decide how many, if any, EL components to use in order to actually save time and money.

EL and the Building Official

The use of EL introduces a whole new level of complication to the building official's job, just as it does to yours. It's best to view the building official as a resource, rather than as an adversary.

When the building official or inspector comes to inspect your framing job, he or she will not just refer to familiar code books. Instead, the inspector will need to check the engineered plot plans and specifications from the EL manufacturer to make sure that you've followed them. In many jurisdictions, you need to submit these documents for review along with your other plans, prior to the issuance of a permit for construction.

Building codes evolve but not as fast as materials and techniques. Also, many sections of the code are open to interpretation. A friendly discussion with your building official can be educational for both of you. He can tell you how other builders are addressing the code and what he expects to see; you can suggest alternatives that you might feel are equivalent or better. Of course, the time to discuss these alternatives is before you use them.

Here are some of the most frequent framing violations, according to my local building official:

■ Missing squash blocks or web stiffeners

■ Missing hardware, especially straps, ties, and hold-downs

■ Damaged or excessively weathered material

■ Improper nailing, either wrong or insufficient nails or sheathing and subflooring nailed with the pneumatic nailer adjusted to an improper depth setting

■ Unreviewed design changes

By far the number one problem he sees, though, is the structural integrity of good framing destroyed by careless or uneducated subcontractors. See chapter 11 for tips on keeping plumbers, electricians, and other subs from damaging the framing.

Fundamental Differences

There are some fundamental principles inherent in EL design and construction that need to be kept in mind as you make the transition from conventional materials and techniques.

Package vs. piecework

Other than the substitution of an EL component for a specific application such as a header, most of our use of EL will be in engineered packages, or systems. For instance, it is common these days for a house to have its floors, its headers, and possibly its roof built from EL, while most of its other parts are conventionally framed. These decisions have structural implications.

Engineering, warranty, and building codes

When building with EL, the engineering, the warranty, and compliance with building codes all depend on using the materials exactly as specified and in conjunction with specific plans. Building codes, for instance, do not include tables for sizing, spacing, and attaching EL materials, as they do for sawn lumber. Instead, there is a blanket provision in most codes that "all materials and components must be used in strict accordance with the manufacturer's specifications."

Warranties from the manufacturer also depend on following these plans and using the specified details. All of the manufacturers provide excellent technical and follow-up support, but they won't help you if you don't follow the rules.

Design Times

Shown here is the Level Design Time for the plot plan on p. 32.

```
            LEVEL NOTES
File Name: 03.0117-ConnellyRyan.JOB
Level Name: Second Floor
Plot Date: 3/3/2003 13:31
Design Date: 3/3/2003 12:32
Drawing Scale: 1/4" = 1'
Job Status:
   Foundation.....Foundation
   Main Floor.....Ready to Plot
                3/3/2003 12:32
   Second Floor...Plotted
                3/3/2003 12:32
   Attic..........Plotted
                3/3/2003 11:47
   Roof...........Plotted
                3/3/2003 11:47

   NOTE: Level design times indicated above
   provide assurance for proper level
   stacking. Upper levels must have earlier
   design times.
Design Methodology: ASD
Floor Area Loads Vary:
   10 to 40 psf Live Load
   10 to 12 psf Dead Load
Maximum Joist Deflection:
   L/480 Live Load
   L/240 Total Load
TJ-Pro Rating Information:
   Weighted Average: 44
   Lowest Rating:   37
   Highest Rating:  60
   Glued & Nailed Decking is Required
   Direct Applied Ceiling of 1/2" Gypsum is
   Required
   Floor Decking: 23/32", 3/4" Weyco Edge
   Gold (24" Span Rating)
Normal O.C. Spacing = 16"*
Default Wall / Beam Width: 5.5"*
Default Header Bearing Length: 1.5"*
Standard Blocking: Bk3*
TJ-Xpert 6.17 (#681) A
C6.17 D6.17 S6.17 P6.17
*Unless noted otherwise
```

Level plans and design times

Level plans and design times are critical. A structure with more than one level constructed with EL, such as one with two floors and a roof, needs to be reviewed and engineered as a whole. Because the load paths are all calculated vertically, the structure will be engineered from the bottom up, and each level will be assigned a design time. They need to be in sequence; in other words, each level must be designed and engineered before the one below it. The levels also must all be part of the same structure and must be referenced to each other. For instance, if you are building a subdivision, you can't apply the same roof plan to houses with different floor plans, even though they may be identical from the exterior.

Making changes

Changes are similarly limited. Any structural, dimensional, or use change needs to go back to the manufacturer for review. For instance, if your client decides to have you finish the space over a garage, the load criteria may change, and this may affect the floor framing, roof framing, and even the wall framing below. The manufacturer will help you with on-site revisions during construction, but because even small changes require review of the entire structural plan, there will be delays.

Selling EL to Customers

Sell the use of EL to your clients during the design stage. Halfway through the project is not the time to find out that your client doesn't believe I-joists will last longer than your warranty. Manufacturers advertise heavily using the concept of improved quality; you can show people these ads. All customers like the idea of speed and efficiency, and some customers are even willing to pay extra for environmental benefits, as well as quality.

Planning for future changes

Just as with conventional framing, you should discuss with your client options for future uses, such as attic finishing, additions, or dormers. The difference with EL is that these possible changes will need to be explained to the engineer so that he can design for them. The plans should specifically note that these design criteria were addressed for future reference.

Engineering differences

Engineers and manufacturers look at the structural performance of an EL system in a way that is fundamentally different from the way they look at standard framing. First, building with EL is much more systemic. You can have an engineer design and size a single EL component, but that is a conventional framing approach. EL is intended to be used in packaged systems. Second, EL systems are entirely vertically supported; there are no triangulated tensile components in an EL system. For instance, a conventional roof might have rafters and collar ties that work together to transfer all of the loads to the outside bearing walls, with the attic joists resisting outward forces and the ridge being primarily nonstructural. An EL roof will always have a structural ridge designed to support half of the rafter load and posts incorporated into the structure to support the ridge. The ceiling joists will not be designed or fastened to resist lateral, or outward, forces.

Lastly, EL components are engineered in conjunction with the hardware that attaches them. While the connections used in conventional framing are determined by building code, tradition, and standard practice, the connections in EL framing are designed, engineered, and specified.

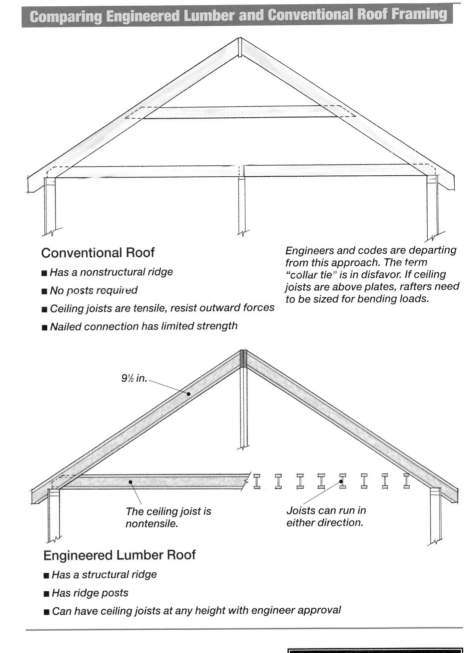

Comparing Engineered Lumber and Conventional Roof Framing

Conventional Roof
- ▪ *Has a nonstructural ridge*
- ▪ *No posts required*
- ▪ *Ceiling joists are tensile, resist outward forces*
- ▪ *Nailed connection has limited strength*

Engineers and codes are departing from this approach. The term "collar tie" is in disfavor. If ceiling joists are above plates, rafters need to be sized for bending loads.

9½ in.

The ceiling joist is nontensile.

Joists can run in either direction.

Engineered Lumber Roof
- ▪ *Has a structural ridge*
- ▪ *Has ridge posts*
- ▪ *Can have ceiling joists at any height with engineer approval*

> **▪ PRO TIP**
>
> **Always keep a copy of all engineered framing plans, and leave a set with the homeowner. These will be critical in designing any future renovation. Using them will be much easier than performing exploratory surgery later.**

While not traditional, the two windows in the gable of this Colonial accommodate the post supporting the structural ridge.

The structural ridge will carry the short rafters on this small addition. There are no joists or collar ties.

Construction techniques

Just as there is a learning curve when designing and planning for use of EL, so too is there a learning curve for the framing crew that actually installs the material. Some manufacturers provide a handy "pocket framer's reference," in some cases attached right to the material. At least the boss and the foreman should read this guide—preferably, the entire crew should. Better yet, everyone on the crew should have their own copy.

Economics

Discounting the expense of the learning curve, every job should get a cost/benefit analysis before moving from conventional to EL framing. In most cases, the material costs for EL will be higher, while the labor costs will be lower. Other costs and benefits are harder to quantify (see

A framing package from TrusJoist includes a dozen or more of these pocket framer's guides. Encased in plastic envelopes attached to the I-joists, each unfolds into a 20-page pamphlet that shows many of the details needed to properly install EL materials.

■ PRO TIP

Although not specifically spelled out by most engineering requirements, interior vertical load paths are good opportunities to build in extra resistance to uplift loads. Some additional hardware can make a much stronger structure.

Cost Benefits

Conventional Framing

■ Familiar

■ Available

■ More weather resistant

■ Less expensive material

■ No unfamiliar or special-order hardware

■ Scrap is more usable/disposable

■ Changes are easier to incorporate

■ Subcontractors are more familiar with the material and can be more easily accommodated

■ Mistakes are more easily fixed

Engineered Lumber

■ Straighter and flatter

■ Stronger

■ No shrinkage

■ Can be used as a selling point for clients

■ Saves labor after initial learning

■ Environmental benefits

■ It's the future—you might as well learn now

the sidebar above). Learning how to build with EL will get you ready for the future when sawn lumber will undoubtedly become more scarce and expensive.

Zone framing

TrusJoist has developed a concept that it calls "Zone Framing." This technique, which utilizes materials in their most efficient locations, is really just a formalization of the decision process that good builders and engineers have been using all along. Primarily intended for wall framing, the Zone Framing (ZF) system identifies key areas in the structure where the benefits of EL material will specifically justify their extra costs.

Tall walls and gables are good candidates for ZF. Long and strong EL materials will make plates and studs in situations where sawn lumber simply can't.

Wind-resistance requirements and large openings will often call for walls that need the extra strength of EL components. Some large walls more closely resemble sideways floor systems because the lateral forces they must resist are similar to the vertical forces exerted on a floor.

Cabinetry calls for walls that are perfectly flat and straight, especially in high-end custom applications. We used to cull or even crown our studs to meet this requirement, but EL is better. Some designers now even specify that the critical walls be framed with EL to eliminate irregularities. Interior finishes such as tile, glass, stone, mirrors, and other exotics can require wall framing that is straighter, stronger, and more stable than conventional sawn lumber. Zone Framing with EL is a good way to address these needs.

Designing for EL

Some of the best buildings I have ever framed were designed by architects who really understood EL; some of the most difficult were EL adaptations of buildings designed for sawn lumber. As with any type of engineering, the best results are achieved by an integrated approach. A structure specifically designed for EL construction will make use of EL's advantages and avoid its limitations.

Joist span and orientation

One of the first surprises when reviewing a set of EL plans is that the joist orientation is often atypical. Whereas a conventionally framed structure will almost invariably have the joists parallel to the rafters, an EL plan will often utilize the greater span capabilities of I-joists by running them in the other direction, thus eliminating a central bearing wall or beam. This saves labor and material and creates a more open floor plan.

Spacing

Designers often take advantage of EL's span characteristics to change joist or rafter spacing, thus saving labor and materials. Whereas most conventional framing today uses 16 in. o.c. as standard, 24 in. o.c. and even 19.2 in. (five bays in 8 ft.) is not unusual in an EL structure. Also, because every part of the structure is analyzed and engineered, often by computer, the joist spacing may change, even within a given area.

Load paths

Load paths, or the transfer of vertical loads down through the structure from the roof to the foundation, are important in any design. EL structures, with their structural ridges and major beams, tend to develop greater loads, especially within the interior of the building. A good plan

Gable Wall Framing

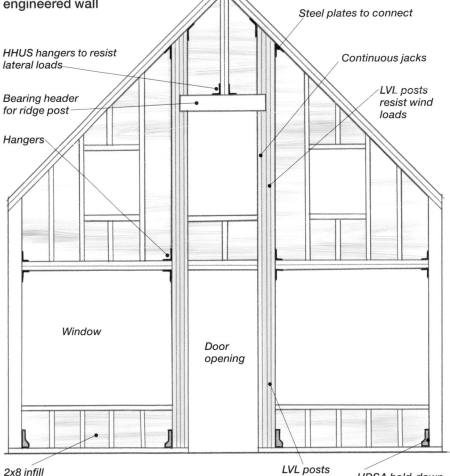

Elevation of a typical engineered wall

- Double LVL plates
- Steel plates to connect
- HHUS hangers to resist lateral loads
- Continuous jacks
- Bearing header for ridge post
- LVL posts resist wind loads
- Hangers
- Window
- Door opening
- 2x8 infill
- LVL posts
- HDSA hold-down

This gable end wall is designed to resist both vertical loading from the ridge post and horizontal loads from 120-mph winds. LVL material is used, with 2x8 dimension lumber as infill framing. Hangers at the intersections around the openings resist lateral forces. The vertical beams created by the double king studs and double trimmers also resist lateral force, as well as carry the header that supports the ridge post.

■ PRO TIP

Watch for areas where joist spacing changes. A floor might have a small section where the layout changes from 16 in. o.c. to 12 in. o.c., perhaps to carry a bay, cantilever, or some upstairs load such as a Jacuzzi. I highlight these areas on the plan using a colored marker.

These plans show the same traditional structure framed two different ways. The conventional method requires central bearing walls or beams. The EL approach allows a more open and flexible floor plan and easier utility runs. Note that the orientation is different and that the joists cannot resist outward forces across the structure. Also note that some or all corners of the stairwell opening are now load bearing.

Conventional floor plan

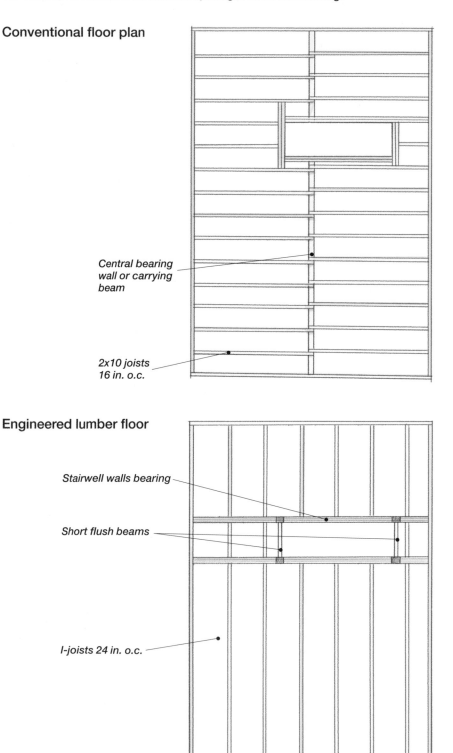

Central bearing wall or carrying beam

2x10 joists 16 in. o.c.

Engineered lumber floor

Stairwell walls bearing

Short flush beams

I-joists 24 in. o.c.

will keep these paths simple and vertically oriented, avoiding lateral transfers of point loads from one level down to the next. Things like openings, utility runs, electrical switching, and plumbing must be considered from the beginning to avoid debacles during construction.

Foundations and footings

The vertically supported load-path engineering of an EL structure can result in much more concentrated point loads than a conventional structure. For example, the greater spans possible with EL girders and I-joists result in more floor area bearing on each Lally column, which may require larger footings. The foundation walls also may take some higher point loads, particularly under the beams and ridge posts. Block foundations in particular may need extra grouting or even pilasters. These calculations need to be done before the foundation is installed (or priced).

Hybridization

Often, there are parts of a structure where framing with EL is advantageous and other areas where it doesn't make sense. In fact, almost every EL structure has major components built of sawn lumber. There are places where the materials can be mixed and places where they can't.

■ Floors should never incorporate sawn lumber and EL together. The differential shrinkage will cause squeaks and bumps later. In fact, this is one of the reasons why manufacturers make I-joists in depths that differ from those of sawn lumber.

■ Walls often incorporate EL components such as headers or plates. The only thing to avoid is a situation where sawn lumber and EL are used to support different parts of the same load. For example, if openings on one side of a room are framed with LVL headers and openings on the other side use 2x12 headers, the joists for the floor above that bear on them will end up out of level when the sawn lumber shrinks and compresses.

■ Roof construction, where shrinkage is not an issue, is the best place for hybrid construction. Building the structural members and large, simple parts of the roof with EL takes advantage of EL's benefits. Building the complex parts of the roof, such as bays and dormers, in sawn lumber avoids the hardware and labor-intensive process of adapting EL components to hips, valleys, jack rafters, and other parts.

■ Interior components such as soffits, built-ins, arches, and substrates for decorative trim are good uses for EL cutoffs and scrap. The material is straight, square, stable, nails well without splitting, and costs nothing.

There is nothing wrong with using EL in renovations. In fact, most older structures being renovated have already undergone most of their shrinkage and settlement, so the stability of EL components is a real asset. For example, joining an addition's new floor made with sawn lumber to the old floor is often problematic: How much will the new floor framing sink? Also, consider that the next renovation will more likely be to the old part of the house, so you might as well build the new part right.

The floor of this addition will meet the old floor perfectly and will stay that way.

▪ PRO TIP

You need to decide on using EL before the foundation is installed, both to get the beam pockets correct and to get the loads calculated.

CHAPTER 5

Working with Engineered Lumber

HIS BOOK IS FOR PROS, so I'll assume that you have a good working knowledge of traditional construction, along with the necessary skills and tools. The next six chapters will emphasize techniques and tools that are specific to EL applications.

Safety First

Construction work is inherently dangerous, second among the major trades only to offshore commercial fishing. A complete treatise on job-site safety is beyond the scope of this book, but there are some concerns specific to engineered materials. Of course, the general concepts are the same as for any type of construction: Keep a clean site; operate high-quality tools in the correct way; use and wear the proper safety equipment; and eliminate distractions so you can stay focused.

PRO TIP

Use web, strap, or even chain binders to temporarily secure stacks of material while they are being moved.

PRO TIP

Never walk between piles that have just been moved. The bands sometimes snap, especially as the ground settles under the load. This can crush legs or worse.

Using hydraulic power to set material on the upper floors is a great time-saver, but be careful.

Handling the material

Many EL components are long, heavy, and slippery. LVLs in particular have a slick coating that allows any unbanded stack to slide apart, often for surprising distances. The long lengths of EL material make many units difficult to balance on the forks of a typical boom truck, crane, or forklift. Manufacturers and lumberyards like to band orders into consistently sized units that store and truck easily, but these units are often comprised of mixed lengths and materials. This makes for a potentially unstable pile, especially as the straps and bands are removed. Be especially cautious when the trucker's straps are removed; if the steel banding has broken in transit, the whole load may slide off. I-joists are often stacked with their flanges offset, which saves space but also makes them likely to leap apart when unbanded.

These I-joists jumped several feet when the last band was cut.

Cutting LVLs generates a cloud of fine granular sawdust.

This slide saw has been retired from trim work and moved to the framing jobs, where it is good for making small and repetitive cuts quickly and safely.

Cutting

Because EL is densely assembled with wood and glue, it tends to produce finer sawdust than most framing materials when cut. This fine sawdust is especially granular because of the glue—which makes it more irritating to the eyes and lungs. Always wear safety glasses when cutting. I don't go so far as to recommend wearing a mask, but I do try to cut outside and to stay upwind.

Aside from the sawdust issue, most EL cuts more easily than sawn lumber because it's dry, straight, and free of grain and internal stress. I-joists are a bit tricky because of their irregular surface; practice your sawing techniques and stay clear of the kickback path. Because many EL components, especially I-joists, are so long and floppy, I use extra sawhorses when cutting them. You can also cut them on the ground or on the pile.

Using stationary tools where possible is safer and saves time, too. I use an old chopsaw on a table for crosscutting small stuff, a slide saw for cutting blocking and web stiffeners, and a small tablesaw for ripping.

Working with LVLs

LVLs are so treacherous that they deserve their own special safety section. Different manufacturers treat and finish their LVLs differently, some better than others, but here are some things to keep in mind. Many LVLs have their edges and ends sealed with a protective wax to keep them from absorbing water. This wax gets on your hammerhead, which makes it slip when driving nails. It also gets on your boots, which makes you slip when you walk. Some LVLs have a paper or plastic facing that makes them even more slippery. Lastly, many framing applications require ripped or beveled edges on structural members. LVLs are good for these applications, but the resulting sharp edges can cut like a knife.

Nailing

Safety glasses should already be part of the job-site uniform, but be especially vigilant about wearing them when nailing into EL hangers. The material is hard and the holes are small, so bent and rebounding nails and fragments are common. Using a pneumatic gun to put 50 or more galvanized nails through a beam hanger can really make the shrapnel fly. Everybody in the vicinity should have glasses on.

Besides hanger nailing, there are two other frequent causes of EL/nailer injuries. The first is nailing I-joist top flanges through a rim joist; because of the small target area and the necessary hand position, getting shot in the left hand or wrist is not uncommon. Another common injury is caused by the hard, slippery covering on LVLs; the nailer slips and the nail is shot into someone beyond the target.

For instructions on installing hangers and other hardware, see chapter 3.

Disposal

On many job sites, scrap wood is burned or buried. Because I'm not sure about the toxicity of the smoke or the ash, I always see that EL scrap goes in a dumpster, where it can be shipped to a landfill. I also put the swept-up sawdust in a dumpster if possible. Of course, treated material should never be burned or buried; this applies to EL as well as to conventional lumber.

Transportation, Care, and Handling of Engineered Lumber

The inherent advantages of engineered lumber—light weight and stability—are best preserved if you take special care in

Using a pneumatic nailer to put 40 to 50 galvanized nails in this hanger generates a lot of flying metal, as well as the plastic and paper from the collated nail strips.

Tacking in a header with a couple of spikes before installing the hangers is fast and efficient, but be careful: A slip or bounce shot here could literally kill you.

▪ PRO TIP

Keeping your EL scrap neatly organized will allow you to make use of many cutoffs, eliminating much of the waste and disposal problem.

▪ PRO TIP

Keep a pile of skids on hand so that when unloading, moving, or restacking EL, you can always make a stack that is straight and level. Pallets also are good for stacking EL components on; they tend to self-level.

handling it at every stage, from delivery to the completion of construction. This process starts when you place the order and continues until you finish the job. A structure built with EL might end up being stronger than a conventional one, but while it is being built, the material is vulnerable to various types of damage and should be protected.

EL needs to be stored flat, straight, and off of the ground and must be kept dry for as long as possible. All forms of EL are dependent on adhesives, and most utilize chips, flakes, strands, or veneers of some sort. These factors make it susceptible to glue failures, dimensional changes, and loss of stability from prolonged cycles of wetting and drying. EL also lacks the natural resilience of sawn lumber; if stacked or stored incorrectly, it can acquire permanent and irreversible bends.

Order wisely

When you place an order for an EL framing package, work with your supplier to arrange for a smooth and timely delivery. Depending on the size and complexity of the job, I usually break the order into packages that utilize the truck's capacity but that also can be installed fairly quickly. For instance, a small house might have a single delivery for the two floors and another load for the roof; a large house might have a delivery for each level. This approach allows me to use leftover materials from the first load and to deduct those materials from my second load's order.

Unloading

As the bundles come off the truck, take the time to get each one supported evenly on a series of skids, typically no more than 8 ft. to 10 ft. apart. Consider the order of installation for the materials. Often, it is most efficient to set beam or ridge stock on top of joist or rafter stock.

Stacking Engineered Lumber Material On Site

Stack material flat and level, making up for differences in ground height by using skids or clubs of scrap lumber. These often come with the load. As often as possible, arrange to put the material you need first on top.

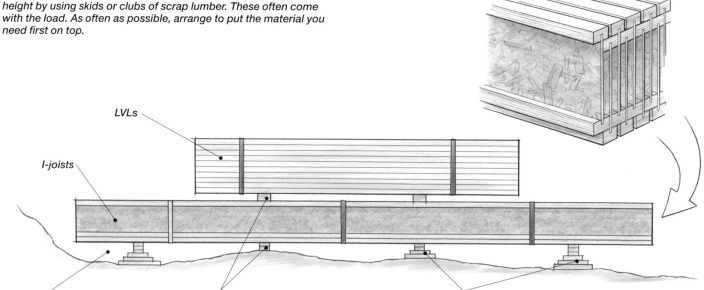

LVLs

I-joists

Avoid ground contact.

Skids for upper pile aligned with lower skids

Stack skids to level support, 8 ft. to 10 ft. maximum.

This saves space, makes it easier to cover, and puts materials at a comfortable working height. Be sure the skids are vertically aligned to prevent deflection, and be careful not to get crushed when cutting the bands on the upper stacks.

Check the quality of the material as you unload. Damage from a forklift or boom that might be inconsequential to sawn lumber can destroy I-joists. Banding that is too tight also can damage I-joists.

Because EL is more expensive and less versatile than sawn lumber, builders tend to return unused material. This is fine, but it means that you might get stuck with a pile that has been weathered for six months or with pieces that have been moved a few times too many. I've had this happen; refusing it might blow your construction schedule but not as badly as a failure to pass your framing inspection.

Handle I-joists gently

With the exception of I-joists, most EL is likely to hurt you if you handle it carelessly. I-joists are delicate until they're installed and should be handled with care. Use enough people so you can move them without excessive bending, and keep them upright as much as possible.

Hydraulic Power Beats Person Power Every Time

Ideally, EL is delivered to the site using a boom or a crane-equipped truck so that it can be placed where it is needed without breaking apart the bundles. I keep the bands on until I need the material; I-joists especially are prone to falling when unbanded. Make sure that there is an adequate flat and clear area for unloading and that you have plenty of skids handy. Try to set down long material oriented in the direction it will be used so you can feed it straight into the house without having to make a large turning radius. Keep the site traffic in mind, too; a couple of 44-ft.-long bundles can really jam up a small site.

The LVLs on top of this stack of material being lifted are slippery and will have a tendency to slide if the load tilts or tips. Adding an extra strap before lifting is inexpensive insurance.

The flange on this I-joist was hit by a forklift, rendering that part of the joist useless.

The first few I-joists in this pile had deep indentations in the flanges, caused by an excessively tight band. This is a good reason to combine short pieces into longer lengths in your order.

Use enough people to lift and move I-joists without excessive bending.

You need four people to send this 42-ft. joist through a window and up to the second floor without bending it too much.

Loading the structure

As you continue to build, be careful how you load additional material into the structure. An I-joist floor or roof can acquire a permanent sag if you overload it with drywall, tile, roofing, or other concentrated loads. Spread the material, load it over beams and bearing walls, or use temporary props below to carry the weight.

Keeping things dry

Once the material is installed in a structure, it's generally not possible to keep it dry. Most jobs get rained on or snowed in a few times between framing and weatherproofing. EL will withstand this, but there are a few steps you can take to help protect it. I drill holes in the subfloor anywhere that water pools, and in the winter, I shovel snow out before it melts. I try to protect the tops of beams with sheathing, felt paper, or glue. I also wrap housewrap into the openings and install pan flashings right away to keep the material around the openings from swelling up and interfering with later finish work.

If the incomplete building will be exposed to a wet climate for a long period, consider temporary coverings over the structure. For that dream home that's going to take five years of weekends to build, you'd better stick to sawn lumber.

This professional-grade 7¼-in. Milwaukee saw has the power and cutting depth to do most tasks, including gang-cutting these rafters.

Tools of the Trade

With a few exceptions, you'll use all of the same basic tools when framing with EL that you would use with conventional lumber. However, there are a few specialized tools as well as site-built jigs that can make the job move more smoothly.

Saws

The job-site workhorse is still the circular saw, either a sidewinder like we use here in the east or one of the worm-drive models that westerners are partial to using. Any professional-grade 7¼-in. saw will do the job, but there are a few things to be aware of. Many standard I-joists have a flange width of 2⁵⁄₁₆ in. to 2⅜ in. This is right at the limit of cutting depth for many saws; if you're going to be cutting a lot of these joists, find a saw that will cut all the way through. Sometimes even a slight difference between blades,

A 12-in. triangular square and Sharpie marker are invaluable, especially for LVLs, which don't take pencil marks well.

Calibrate a 50- or 100-ft. Tape

Most long tapes (50 ft. or 100 ft.) are not designed for the precision carpentry that custom framers like to do. Check the end hooks against a standard tape and make adjustments as needed. When using a nonsteel tape, be careful of stretch.

such as between a new blade and a resharpened one, will affect the cutting depth. For gang cutting, bevel cutting, or for larger flanges, an 8¼-in. saw is well worth having, although most of us prefer not to use these heavier saws on an everyday basis unless we have to. (Even larger saws, such as those often used by timber framers, are available but are not necessary for most framing jobs.)

Measuring and marking tools

Just as with sawn lumber, we measure EL with a tape and mark it with a pencil and a square. EL requires a bit more technology, though. The average tape measure we typically carry in our tool belts maxes out at 30 ft. or 35 ft., which is not long enough for many EL components. A 50-ft. or 100-ft. steel tape is a real help. A standard carpenter's pencil is fine for I-joists, LSLs, and rim joist stock but worthless on many LVLs and PSLs. A black marker is better, especially for layout work. I like the Sharpie® brand of permanent marker; I carry a thin one for marking and a fat one for layout, for cautions to subs, and for other miscellaneous notes on the material. The triangular square, introduced by Swanson Speed Line Tools® as the Speed Square, has revolutionized frame carpentry, but for EL, the larger 12-in. model is necessary. An old-fashioned framing square can substitute, but it's not nearly as convenient.

Nailing tools

According to the engineers, most EL is no harder than the average piece of softwood framing lumber. In practice, however, the glue, the density, and the lack of grain often make the material so hard that hand nailing it can be an exercise in frustration. For the nails you do need to drive by hand, use a 23-oz. or heavier

Pneumatic Nailers

Efficient framing with EL often requires using at least four nailers at once. For instance, installing web stiffeners and hangers on both ends of long rafters is best accomplished with a spike gun (a standard pneumatic gun) and a hanger gun at each end. If a second crew is simultaneously installing the rafters as they are prepped, that's two more guns. For these reasons, and because of breakdowns, I generally have at least six nailers set up at any given time, even on a modest-size framing job.

For spikes (12d) and ring-shanks (8d), I keep a fleet of coil nailers. They are of several different makes, but they all shoot the same nails. Most framers I know prefer coil nailers to stick nailers because they hold more nails and are more compact. Stick nailers are lighter, though, and I have several that I use when I need to hold the nailer over my head for extended periods.

For hanger nails, I use the Paslode Positive Placement Nailer, but there are other good choices as well. I generally have two in use, plus a spare; these nailers have complicated mechanisms doing a brutal job and consequently are prone to failure. I've found that the key to success with these is keeping the paper-collated nails crisp, dry, and gently handled.

Stanley®Bostich makes a convertible stick nailer that will shoot regular framing nails or hanger nails by switching magazines. For the carpenter who needs to limit his nailer ownership, this versatility is probably a good deal.

Features I look for in a nailer are power, durability, reliability, easy jam clearing, and a good belt hook. For nailing sheathing, a good depth adjustment is crucial as well. The keys to getting reliable service from nailers are daily oiling and keeping dirt and dust out of the hoses and mechanisms.

This nailer converts from framing nails to hanger nails by switching magazines.

These are the nailers I would typically have in use on a framing job with a small crew.

I keep three of these nailers on hand—two to use and one as a spare.

This 25-oz. framing hammer has the weight to do the job efficiently and to knock components into alignment. The serrated face resists slipping, especially when using wax-covered LVLs.

Narrow I-joists like these can be cut accurately by aiming the guide mark on the saw toward a mark on the opposite flange.

framing hammer, preferably with a serrated or waffle-faced head.

For most fastening tasks, use a pneumatic nailer. Not all nailers have enough power; I've retired several that couldn't consistently set 12d or 16d nails all the way into EL material. Because of the number of metal fasteners involved, you really should have a separate pneumatic nailer for hanger nails as well.

Techniques of the Trade

Most of the general techniques used with EL are the same as those with sawn lumber. However, each specific type of EL material has its own nuances.

Cutting and nailing I-joists

I-joists are the mainstay of most EL floor and roof systems, so naturally they're the most difficult components to work with. First, they're not shipped in a flat stack that you can cut on directly, and they're not easy to pick up and set on sawhorses. The best technique is to lift several at a time from the edge to the top of the pile and cut them there.

In addition, I-joists are not flat sided, which makes them hard to mark. Often, neither end is square. I often check to see if one end of the stack has better ends; if they're close to square, I use them, but I make sure I'm measuring from the longer flange on an out-of-square end. When working with smaller I-joists, such as 9½ in. or 11⅞ in., I only mark the flanges. I find that I can cut them accurately enough by aiming the saw guide notch at the mark on the far flange. Wider I-joists need to be marked across the flange, either by using a small square or by making a marking jig (see p. 55). Some carpenters use either a square or a jig as a hand-held saw guide.

A simple jig both squares the cut and supports the saw base.

More complicated cuts, such as bird's-mouth and tail cuts, really should be marked using a jig (see p. 55). When making notched or angled cuts in I-joists, check the manufacturer's literature for allowable details. There are restrictions on the amount of flange material that can be notched or cut and on overcutting within the webs. I-joists with flanges wider (that is, thicker) than your saw can cut are especially challenging. Square cuts can be made by rolling the saw up one edge and down the other. For angled cuts, you really have no choice but to flip the I-joist over and finish the cut from the other side. Good support and maybe some help on the other end is crucial here; either support the I-joist at several points, or have a helper hold the waste side while you cut.

Nailing I-joists requires attention to the manufacturer's specification, as well as careful aim. Nailing through a rim joist into the top flange of an I-joist needs to be done carefully to avoid missing the

Many carpenters use their 12-in. triangular square as a guide for making square cuts.

flange or shooting over the top. The toe-nails through the bottom flange have to be angled carefully to avoid splitting; this is especially troublesome with lumber flanges, which is why I prefer laminated or stranded flanges.

Cutting and nailing LVLs

LVL stock often arrives on site looking as though it was cut to shipping length with a chainsaw. More subtle, but equally problematic, is the flare that often occurs in the last foot or so of a factory end. I've often found that the end of an 11⅞-in. LVL is flared along one or both edges to as much as 12¼ in. wide. This will make an awful bump if you don't catch it and saw it off. Check the ends for both

These LVLs were nailed together using a nailer, but it takes the weight of a big hammer to get them tight together.

LVLs often need to be gang-nailed together to create built-up members. This requires pounding them with a big hammer; I often shoot the nails in with a nailer and use the hammer to tighten them as I go.

LSLs, PSLs, and rim joists

In contrast to the other EL materials, this stuff is a pure pleasure to work with. It cuts and nails easily—just like sawn lumber but better since it doesn't split, twist, or bind. The only drawback is the size and weight of some of the pieces, but this is its advantage, too. Cut it on the ground or on the pile, and use hydraulic, mechanical, or person power to set it in place.

squareness and width, and trim them in both directions as required. If you don't have the length to chop the flare off the end, you'll need to rip it off the edge.

Use a felt-tipped marker on LVLs; pencil marks are almost invisible. Most sawblades tend to wander when ripping LVLs, so if you need to rip, use a sharp blade and go slowly. A heavy blade takes more time and power, but it tends to make a straighter rip than the thin-kerf blades most of us are framing with these days.

Sliding the beam off the end of the pile and cutting it there saves time and energy, especially for young carpenters with good backs.

Site-Built Jigs

A site-built jig makes work proceed more smoothly and helps you produce more accurate cuts. I-joists and rafters especially benefit from the use of jigs.

I-joist jigs

Generally, jigs are useful for I-joists because they don't have a flat surface. Narrow I-joists can be marked and cut by just using the flanges, but it's difficult to get the line to match up with the lines on the flanges, so wider I-joists need some sort of marking on the web. You can draw freehand across the web using the square as a guide, but many framers make a simple jig. A scrap of plywood the width of the I-joist and nailed to a scrap of web stiffener material is the easiest. This jig can be used for both marking and cutting, and with a bit of customizing, it can be used to cut directly without marking a square line first.

Rafter jigs

A cutting jig for rafters uses the same concept and construction as any other I-joist jig. The difference is that it is set up for top cuts, bird's mouths, or tail cuts. Generally, one short jig is made that serves for both ends. If the rafters have been stacked and gang-cut, the jig is just used to complete the marks. Otherwise, reference marks are used to establish lengths.

Rafter patterns

An EL roof will often incorporate rafters made of different materials, such as LVLs or LSLs, in addition to the I-joist commons. In a simple structure, there are many identical rafters, and if they can't be gang-cut, a pattern rafter is helpful. A spare piece of rim joist makes a straight, light pattern. An LVL makes a heavy, slippery pattern, but if you use one of the rafters that you need to make anyway, it's efficient. Otherwise, a pattern can be made from several scraps nailed to a 2x4 or from dimension lumber. Keep in mind, though, that the different rafter types may have different hardware, and allowances may need to be made for the various flange thicknesses.

The flanges on this hanger require this end of the rafter to be shortened about ³⁄₁₆ in.

Made for I-joist rafters, this jig incorporates both a plumb cut and the bird's mouth and tail. It was made with a piece of ½-in. plywood nailed to web stiffener material.

CHAPTER 6

Beams and Girders

THE LARGE STRUCTURAL MEMbers that typically support floor structures are normally called "girders" by engineers and "carrying beams" by carpenters. They often span the entire length or width of the house, providing midspan support for floor joists. These beams also support bearing walls and columns in the upper levels of the structure. Often a carrying beam will be placed under the transition from one part of a house to another, such as where a wing joins the main section. Beams made from engineered lumber are a tremendous improvement over traditional dimensional timbers or built-up beams made by nailing together 2x material. In fact, EL carrying beams are often incorporated into otherwise conventionally framed structures.

These completed beams are ready for joists.

Typical EL Floor Plan

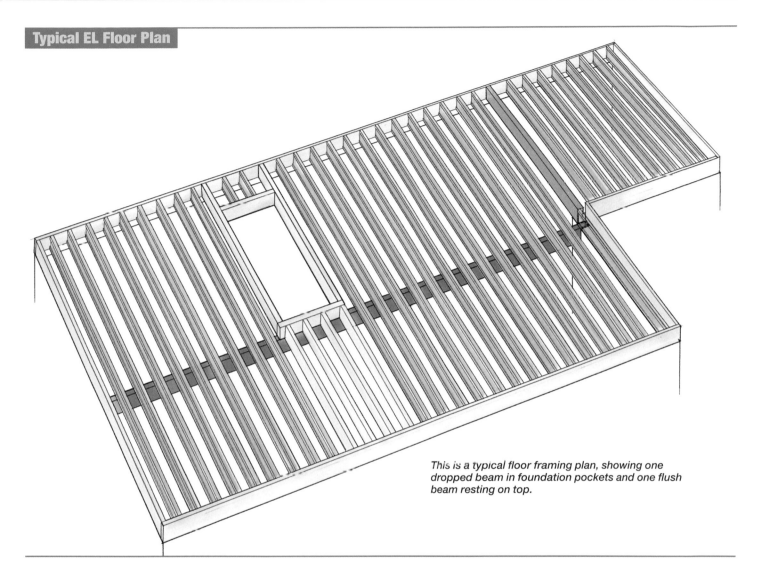

This is a typical floor framing plan, showing one dropped beam in foundation pockets and one flush beam resting on top.

Types of Carrying Beams

Most carrying beams are hidden in a basement or crawl space, so their selection is purely utilitarian—whichever material is most available, easiest to install, and will do the structural job most efficiently and economically. Occasionally, a house will have a carrying beam in a visible location. Architectural-grade glulams have been the traditional choice here, although I know of one builder who used PSL beams in his own house; he likes the industrial look they took on when he finished them with polyurethane.

Using an Engineered Beam in a Sawn Lumber Floor

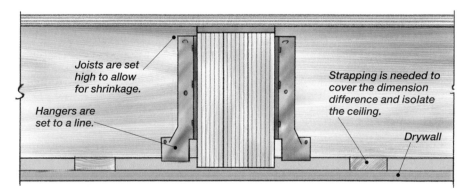

Joists are set high to allow for shrinkage.

Hangers are set to a line.

Strapping is needed to cover the dimension difference and isolate the ceiling.

Drywall

We often use an EL beam in a conventionally joisted floor. With a little attention to detail, this is an excellent and economical practice.

The PSLs were cleaned, sanded, and polyurethaned for a different look. Note the custom-made industrial-strength hardware.

One stick or many?

As with conventional lumber, you have a choice between dropping one big beam into place or assembling a beam from multiple smaller pieces. Sometimes the choice of material dictates this. For example, parallel strand beams are usually ordered at full thickness rather than built up on site; LVLs by their nature need to be assembled into beams on site. Often the engineer decides for you: Just use whatever is specified. In general, a single large beam is more efficient if you can use a crane or boom truck to set it in place; assembled beams are easier for the typical small framing crew. The overall length of the beam, its location within the structure, and site or schedule constraints are some of the factors that will influence this decision.

Flush or dropped?

Carrying beams can be "dropped beams," which are installed below the level of the joists, or "flush beams," which are installed in the same plane as the joists. Sometimes, where the beam dimension is larger than the joist dimension, they are both. Dropped beams are faster and easier in most cases. They do require pockets in the walls or foundation, but the joists run right over them in continuous lengths. However, they reduce the overhead clearance in the room below. Most of the sub trades find dropped beams easier to work with because the bays between joists are open; the exception is in a basement where a long sewer or HVAC trunk line needs to run under the joists and cross the beams. Flush beams are labor and hardware intensive, but they preserve headroom and the plane of the ceiling below.

Architectural-grade glulams span 24 ft. across this house.

Beam Sections

Flush Beam

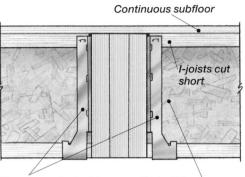

Continuous subfloor

I-joists cut short

Hangers on both sides

Web stiffeners sometimes required

Pros:

- Fits within the floor system to maximize headroom or maintain an unbroken ceiling plane
- Rests on walls; no beam pockets
- Solid bearing surface for point loads

Cons:

- Drilling limitations restrict utility rows
- Labor intensive; more cutting and nailing
- Hangers often protrude below the framing plane
- Prone to squeaks

Beam Both Flush on Top and Dropped on Bottom

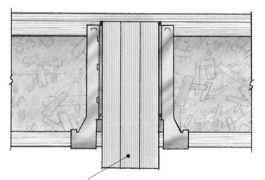

Hangers set to snapped lines

The worst of both worlds; all of the disadvantages of both types of beams. Use only when the depth required for the span can't be fit within the floor.

Dropped Beam

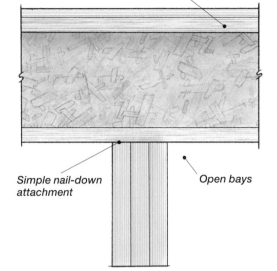

Both joists and subfloor are continuous.

Simple nail-down attachment

Open bays

Pros:

- Continuous joists are faster, stronger, and less prone to squeaks
- Generally less labor intensive
- Beam location can be less than precise
- Easier utility and insulation runs

Cons:

- Less headroom below
- Requires a foundation or frame pockets
- Can interfere with trunk or soil lines
- Often requires squash blocks or blocking panels
- Beam often needs to be wrapped

■ PRO TIP

With good preparation and organization, you can climb onto the boom truck that delivers the beam, cut it to length, and have it set right in place. To save both crew time and crane time, you don't want to move it twice. If you're asking the truck driver to wait while you do this, using a chainsaw is a handy way to speed the process. Just work carefully.

■ **PRO** TIP

Make sure that any wall incorporating a column or post is thick enough to conceal it; otherwise it will need to be furred out later.

A flush beam carries joists in both directions, preserving the ceiling plane through the hallway.

The end of this carrying beam is supported by a post made of five 2x6s. The beam end is notched so that the wall plates can run through; the stud next to the post and beam aids assembly and prevents twist.

Supporting the Beam

A carrying beam under the first floor of a structure is typically supported at the ends by beam pockets in the foundation and at intermediate points by columns, usually cement-filled steel Lally columns on concrete footings. If the beam goes through or over an intersecting wall, it is generally supported by a post in the wall made of multiple jack studs. Sometimes an engineered column or steel post is specified to be incorporated into the wall. The two critical issues here are bearing lengths and underlying supports.

Bearing lengths

Bearing length refers to the area of the beam that must rest on its support. Area, of course, is in square inches, but because the width of the beam is a constant, the area can be specified by length. The total load on the beam including its own weight, divided by the number of square inches it rests on, gives a compressive load in pounds per square inch (psi). This value must be within the allowable standards for the material that the beam is made from. The engineered plan will always specify required bearing lengths at the end and intermediate supports for carrying beams, as well as for joists and headers. These are usually given in a table or list, with a minimum bearing length to be maintained anywhere that specific longer lengths are not shown. These values are important; a beam pocket that is only half as deep as required will double the compressive load on the end of the beam, significantly increasing the chance that the beam will fail when the weights of finish materials and furniture have been added later.

Beam pockets

The ends of first-floor carrying beams typically rest in beam pockets in the foundation wall. These pockets need to be sized and located correctly. The width needs to accommodate the beam with code-required airspace (typically ½ in.) on either side. The height should ideally have the top of the beam flush with the mudsills. The depth should provide the required bearing length, plus airspace at the end of the beam. Finally, the location should place the beam correctly in the structure, especially when there is an opening adjacent to it.

Intermediate supports

Intermediate supports for beams will be specified as well. These will be columns or posts sized to carry the compressive loads; there will also be a specified bearing length. In most cases, the top of the column itself will not be large enough, so a block, steel plate, or column cap will be required. Most codes now require built-up carrying beams, whether conventional or EL, to be contained and supported by column caps. LCC-type caps address both the code and the bearing requirements.

Because EL beams are stronger, the supports are often farther apart. This may mean that larger footings, or pads, are required. Sometimes, these point loads require additional reinforcing in or on top of the concrete as well.

The location of this stair opening requires that the carrying beam be precisely located with reference to the floor plan.

Lally column caps contain and control both the column and the beam.

Beam Pockets: the Good, the Bad, and the Ugly

Beam pockets, whether formed or cut into a concrete wall or incorporated into a masonry wall, need to be sized correctly. Foundation contractors are notorious for messing this up; after all, they are not framers, and they'll be long gone before you and your lumber show up. Here are some things you can do to forestall problems.

Try to have the engineered plan completed before building the foundation so that the depths, widths, and bearing lengths of the beams are known. Most codes require clearance for airspace between the concrete and the beam, usually ½ in. on either side and at the end. The form workers like tapered pockets because they are easier to strip. That's fine, but you need to make sure the dimension required is the smallest part of the pocket, not just the size at the front.

The distance from the top of the foundation to the bottom of the pocket is important. In an ideal world, the foundation will be flat, and the beam will sit flat in the pocket on a piece of sill seal, with its top flush with the mudsills. In the real world, some trimming or shimming is usually required. There are generally allowable or required materials for this. You can use steel plates, solid masonry materials, or treated wood blocks, subject to grain and minimum size. For the inevitable situation where a pocket needs to be enlarged, a small angle grinder with a diamond blade is essential. Don't use a hammer drill and chisel bit, as this can leave fracture lines in the masonry.

Anatomy of a Good Beam Pocket

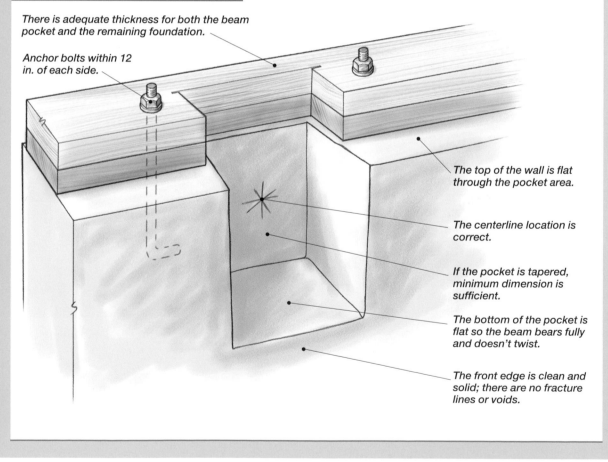

There is adequate thickness for both the beam pocket and the remaining foundation.

Anchor bolts within 12 in. of each side.

The top of the wall is flat through the pocket area.

The centerline location is correct.

If the pocket is tapered, minimum dimension is sufficient.

The bottom of the pocket is flat so the beam bears fully and doesn't twist.

The front edge is clean and solid; there are no fracture lines or voids.

Installing Lally Column Caps (LCCs) onto a Built-Up Beam

Lally caps are much easier to install before you finish building the beam. Assuming that you haven't messed up and already assembled your carrying beams in place, here's how to install these critical components.

1. Start with the first member of the built-up beam in place. Mark the locations where the columns will support the beam, making sure they are roughly centered on the footings below.

2. Loosely tack the column cap in place with a couple of nails, letting it hang to one side.

3. Lift the Lally column into place, top first, and plumb it in both directions. (You already calculated the lengths and precut all of the Lally columns, right?)

4. Finish assembling the beam within the cap.

There are alternate techniques. Some carpenters install all of the columns and caps with temporary braces and build the beam right in the caps. Others build the beam in place but block up a few inches to allow installation of the columns. These methods work too, and you may prefer them.

■ PRO TIP

Many framers build carrying beams on temporary supports and put the Lally columns in later. When using LCCs, don't do this. There is not enough side clearance in the collar to get the column in without jacking up the beam.

Lally columns are lifted into the caps and plumbed.

Sometimes the LCC needs to be spread to slip the last ply into it.

First, spike the LVLs together using a heavy hammer, until there is no space between them. Sometimes I set a few nails using a nailer and drive them tight with the hammer.

As the beam is assembled, nail it together with spikes according to the engineer's or manufacturer's schedule. Four nails through every layer every 16 in. would not be unusual.

Assembling and Installing Beams

A beam that consists of one piece can be cut to length and dropped into place. A built-up beam can be preassembled and dropped into place too, depending on the size of the beam and the size of the crew. The key in these cases is accurate prep work: The beam must be accurately cut to length, and the supports must be correctly placed and firmly braced.

More often, the carrying beam is made up of multiple layers of LVL, which are slid into place and spiked together. (This process is the same as for conventional lumber beams, except that the components are usually longer, often full length.) The material supplier or the engineered plan will provide a fastening schedule, which is usually a nailing spec and pattern but sometimes includes lags or bolts.

Two or three members can be assembled and nailed together in one step; four or more members need to be nailed as they are assembled. The nailer is king for this tough stuff but beware. Be sure to spike each piece together using a big hammer first. If you put all the nails in while there is still airspace between the members, they are virtually impossible to tighten up later. The beam also needs to be straight; if you get it all nailed together with a curve from side to side, the beam will resist any later attempts to straighten it out.

Assembling a typical beam

The beam shown in this sequence is a typical assembly of LVLs under the first floor of a small house. Made of four 1¾-in. by 9½-in. LVLs, it is efficient to buy and to build, while preserving headroom and floor space in the basement. The equivalent beam in conventional lumber

Types of EL Carrying Beams

There are four choices for EL carrying beams: LVL, PSL, glulam, and LSL. For the few situations where one of these choices will not suffice, most engineers turn to steel—either an I-beam or a flitch beam (see p. 68).

LVLs are the most common choice for carrying beams. They are a standard 1¾-in. thickness and come in depths ranging from 7¼ in. to 16 in. They are assembled in combinations of two, three, or four layers, producing beam thicknesses of 3½ in., 5¼ in., or 7 in., respectively. Because the individual pieces are smaller and more manageable, they can be assembled into tremendously long and strong beams by a small crew without hydraulic power.

PSLs are a good choice for carrying beams. They are available in widths from 1¾ in. to 7 in. and in depths from 9¼ in. to 18 in. They are rated as slightly stronger than built-up LVL assemblies and are available pressure treated, making them suitable for damp crawl spaces and exterior applications. Their size and weight is a mixed blessing. If you can have a crane or boom truck set a single 7-in. by 18-in. by 36-ft.-long beam, it's fast, strong, and economical. If you need to set it with human power, you're better off with an assembled beam.

Glulams are the usual choice for beams that are exposed to view and finished. They are available in clean, sanded architectural grades, which, if protected during construction, finish beautifully. They are available in virtually any size and shape you might want, including curved arches and massive beams large enough to span small rivers.

LSLs are a rare choice for carrying beams, not because they would be inappropriate but because other choices are better. Because of their clean shape and dimensional stability, they are more often used for headers within floor or wall systems.

PRO TIP

Many framers set conventional carrying beams slightly high to allow for shrinkage and compression. Don't do this with engineered lumber, as it will cause a bump in the floor later.

would be 2 in. deeper, and the columns would be 7 ft. apart instead of 9 ft.

1. Check the pockets and column footings for size, depth, and location. Set up a taut string, either at the center of the beam location as shown in the top photo on p. 66 or along one edge. Next, pull the string taut enough to measure the height of the columns. I add a little bit, perhaps ⅛ in. in the middle of a 32-ft. span, to allow for string sag and column base compression.

2. Measure the column lengths. Take the height from the footing to the top of the mudsills, and subtract the beam depth and the thickness of the plates

on either end of the column. Cut and label the columns.

3. Measure the length of the beam, allowing for end clearance in the pockets but maintaining the required bearing lengths. Cut the beam members to length, and clear a path for sliding them into place from one end.

4. Muscle the first piece into place, bracing it if necessary to keep it from flopping over and out of its pockets.

5. Slide each successive piece out along the top of the beam, and roll it into place from the ends. Nail the layers together as you go.

A string run along the centerline of the beam provides measurements for the columns. The notch in the plate locates the beam precisely and also allows measurement of the beam length. When the beam is in place, the string is reset slightly higher and is used to straighten the beam.

Assembling a spliced beam

The length of the LVL stock that you make your beams with is limited by your ability to transport, store, and handle it. In most areas, that means about 44 ft., which will make full-length carrying beams for most applications. Occasionally, though, a beam needs to be spliced. Just as with conventional framing, the splices must be located over the supports. (This is the easiest approach to design and build and the method most engineers and building officials will specify, even though the strongest beam will have some of the splices at the points of zero moment load instead of over the posts.) The only difference in assembly technique is the additional bracing required during the process.

Put the slippery edge of the LVLs to work when you slide successive pieces into place. The perpendicular LVL will be the last ply; it rests on sawhorses and is used to support the LVL being slid.

Carrying Beams

Beam with Splices over Supports

Splice

Maximum moment or bending splice

Bending stress

Continuous Beam

Point of zero moment

A long carrying beam can be continuous or spliced. If it is built of multiple plies, the different layers should be spliced at different locations. A continuous beam is stronger because the maximum moment, or bending, loads on it are smaller. Of course, that's not the whole story: Beams also need to resist shear and compression loads,

most beams carry point loads, and even the uniform loads and spans are not evenly distributed. The strongest beam will have its splices precisely engineered and located. However, most engineers simply size the beams for the worst-case scenario and call for a discontinuous beam with joints directly over each of its supports.

Flush beams

Flush beams can be built and installed using most of the same techniques that are used for drop beams. There are a few extra considerations and opportunities, though. Occasionally, a flush beam is used in a first floor, where it simply rests on the sills. More often, flush beams are used in upper floors, where headroom or a ceiling plane must be maintained. In either case, figure out whether the hardware requires cutting mortises or making any other modifications to the beam to prevent the hardware from interfering

with finishing the floors and ceilings later. Also, check carefully that no plumbing or other utility access through the bays will be blocked.

Flush beams can often be set in place with the hangers already installed. This can include not only hangers for the joists that will be attached to the beam but also the end hangers that carry the beam itself. On big and heavy beams, I don't generally preinstall hangers because of the danger to the crew if the beams slip while being lifted into place.

Steel Beams

There are two approaches to using steel in an EL structure. An I-beam is a common choice for a carrying beam or a ridge where exceptional strength or span is needed. It's useful to have a copy of *Handbook of Steel Sections and Properties*, which provides exact dimensions and properties. For instance, a W12x36 is an I-beam 12⅛ in. deep with a 5¼-in. flange width, weighing 36 lb. per linear foot. The other, less common approach is a flitch beam, made by sandwiching a steel plate between two pieces of wood.

I-beams can be used as they are shipped, by ordering them cut to length, and welding top flanged hangers on them for the joists, although most framing crews are not equipped for on-site welding and prefer not to use this method. More often, a piece of wood material is bolted to the flange, which the hangers are then nailed on to. If the beam is to be wrapped with finish materials, it helps to bolt a plate to the bottom as well, provided the headroom will allow it. Order the beam with all of the holes predrilled; you don't want to do it on site. Sometimes, an engineer will design a system wherein you need to bolt lumber pieces onto the sides of the web. This is so labor-intensive and inefficient that it's worth going back to the engineer to design an alternate system if possible.

Flitch beams are assembled with two pieces of EL or lumber bolted on either side of a steel plate. A fastening schedule will show the number, size, and pattern of the bolts. Order the plate with all of the holes drilled. Set the two pieces of lumber on a flat surface, lay the plate on top, and drill straight down through it and through the two wood pieces. Without changing the orientation of any of the pieces, slip the plate between the two lumber pieces; all of the holes should line up. Flitch beams generally require bearing plates to take the load from the edge of the plate to the bearing column or surface; allow for these when aligning the members. Also, it's important to plan for your joist layout so that the bolt heads don't get in the way. Otherwise, you'll have to shift your layout, notch your joists, or both.

I once built from a set of plans that included two 20-ft. flitch beams, each made of three 2x12s with two ¾-in. by 11-in. steel plates, all through-bolted. These mighty beams were designed to hold up primarily interior coffered ceiling details. When I questioned the designer, he admitted to not knowing quite how to calculate the loads, which he compensated for by substantial overengineering. I showed him how to do the calculations, and in the process demonstrated that these two beams, adequately supported, would hold up the ferryboat that comes to our island!

The steel I-beams under this floor preserve headroom and increase span, while keeping the bays open. Note the pilastered block foundation.

Ways to Use Steel I-Beams and a Flitch Beam

2x6 bolted on top (preferred method)

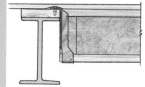

- Top-mounted flange is required
- Sometimes backing is required
- Sometimes strapping along the bottom will eliminate the need for backing (ask an engineer)

Welded-on flanges (alternate method)

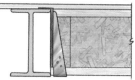

- Simple, clean system
- Need welder
- No fastening for subflooring

Through-bolted ledger stock with face-mounted hangers

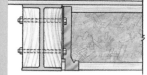

- Strong but time-consuming

Flitch beam: steel plate bolted between 2xs

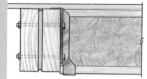

- Strong, easy to finish
- Uses any type of hanger
- May need bearing plates

Finishing the Installation

When the carrying beam is assembled and in place, it needs to be straightened, checked for level, and secured in position. Check for level by using a transit, laser, or standard carpenter's level or by reference to the mudsills. To check for straightness, eye it carefully or use a string along one corner. Also, check for the beam's position in the structure, especially if it forms one side of an opening such as a stairwell. Temporary braces can hold the beam laterally, or the first few joists can be set in place and nailed. Short pieces of metal strapping can be used to secure the ends to the sills.

Height issues need to be addressed now, before loading the beam. If intermediate supports are too high, they can be trimmed; if too low, they can be replaced or shimmed. The shims should be steel plates that will handle the compressive loads without bending or deforming, and they should have at least the area of the required bearing surface to prevent the beam from failing in compression or shear.

Preinstalling this end hanger on the beam will make it easy to secure in position with a couple of nails.

A flush beam is lifted into place with its hangers already installed.

CHAPTER 7

Floors—Faster and Flatter

FLOOR FRAMING WAS ONE OF the original applications for complete engineered lumber systems, and it's still where these materials really shine. An engineered floor system is easier and faster to build than a conventionally framed floor, and the finished product is straighter, stronger, and flatter.

Designing the System

The engineering of a structure built with EL is based primarily on the floor systems and to a lesser extent on the roof system. All of the other components, such as carrying beams, headers, and columns, are dependent on the design of these primary systems.

Typical Floor Plan

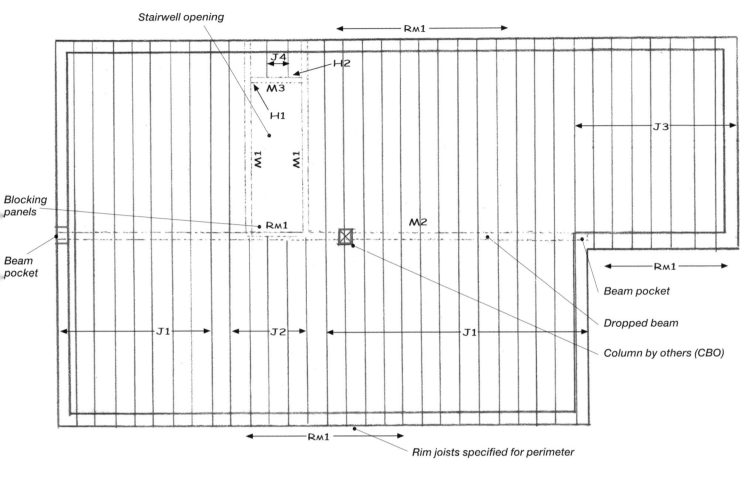

This is a typical floor framing plan from an EL manufacturer. In combination with the manufacturer's framing guide, it contains all of the information necessary to assemble the system.

Engineered floor systems begin with a design provided by the manufacturer of the products. You would then give the blueprints for the structure to your lumber supplier, along with information about the code and load requirements. The supplier in turn passes this information to the engineered lumber manufacturer, who uses proprietary software to produce a computer-aided design (CAD) drawing for each of the floors. These drawings come back from the supplier with a list of materials and a price quote. Interestingly, different manufacturers and engineers will find very different approaches to building the same structure. Unless you are loyal or limited to one supplier, it's worth getting designs and quotes from several.

Checking the design

The software used for the design of floor systems is a well-developed and mature technology, but, like all computer systems, it's only as good as the information fed into it. If the original prints are not clear or if the person inputting the data misinterprets them, the floor design will not fit the structure. I've found that time invested here is well spent and that several

This double LVL header fits in a 2x4 wall and carries the second floor across the opening.

revisions to the design are not unusual, especially with complex structures.

The plot plans coming back from the manufacturer are often not to the same scale as the blueprints and are sometimes not to any specific scale that you can use. Write the important measurements on the plot plan, or create a custom scale for use with that particular plan. I do this by setting a piece of cardboard along a simple dimension on the plan, such as the side of a floor that I know is 24 ft. long. I then divide that length into single feet on the cardboard and mark them.

1. Check the critical dimensions and openings. Standard items like stairwells and chimney holes are usually correct, but sometimes a design will miss details such as cathedral ceiling areas, skylight wells, or cantilevers.

2. Check the bearing walls and columns. Usually the only walls shown on the plot plan are the ones assumed to be bearing. Make sure that all of these are correct and can be built as bearing walls. If there is an opening in the wall, make sure that there is room for an adequate header and that the required header is specified. Make sure that any columns are correctly placed in the plan and that they can be incorporated into a wall if necessary. If a bearing wall or column needs to accommodate plumbing, check the drilling restrictions and size or furr the wall accordingly.

3. Check ledger attachment areas. Most houses have porches or decks, and these generally need ledgers attached to the outside walls. An I-joist won't do; change it to something solid such as a rim joist or LSL. No manufacturer that I've worked with ever does this without your input.

4. Check for construction efficiency. The software will optimize the plan to min-

imize material costs, but it doesn't factor in labor costs. For instance, a beam made by doubling I-joists might be less expensive to buy, but experience will tell you that if you need to pad out the webs to accommodate joist or beam hangers, it's more efficient to use an LVL instead.

5. Check the plumbing, both the fixture locations and the pipe runs.

6. Check the materials list. The software will provide an itemized list of materials needed for each floor, including the hardware. You can order this as a package, and it will usually be exactly right. However, I've learned to combine some of the lengths into longer pieces in the order so that a cutting mistake won't leave me short. Also, blocking panels, which are short sections of I-joist, can be ordered as long pieces instead of shorts, giving you an additional margin for error.

In addition, check the hardware list. Most of the hangers are standard, but occasionally custom or special-order hardware is specified, which may need to be ordered weeks earlier than the rest of the package. Sometimes, the software will specify a piece of hardware as "not found," which means that it's necessary but unavailable, and some creative reengineering is required (see chapter 3).

Supporting the Floor

Just as with conventional framing, an engineered floor needs to be built on flat, level, and square sills, walls, and beams. Prepare and brace the bearing walls using levels and string lines. Make sure that beams are straight and flat, that sills are shimmed and bolted down, and that all columns are in place to support flush beams in the floor system. None of this is

Planning the Plumbing

Design software is great at locating things like toilet flanges and moving joists accordingly, but it doesn't understand where the pipes go from there. A toilet flange or shower drain that sits neatly between two joists will do you no good if it is boxed in between flush beams and cannot reach a wall to get down to the basement, or if a dropped beam forces the pipe below the level of the sewer main.

To make sure that all of the pipes will fit, will run downhill, and can remain hidden within the floor system, you need to review the plan carefully with your plumber. Sometimes a structural design revision will solve problems at this stage. In other cases, you might have to get creative with soffits, dropped ceilings, or furred walls. Sometimes, an architect will design a house that just can't be plumbed.

Watch for nonstandard tub and shower designs. The software assumes that all tubs drain from one end and all showers from the center. This is not always true, and mistakes can be tough to fix. Corner showers are all different, so their drain locations need to be field verified.

any different than preparing for a conventional floor, but it can be more difficult to adjust things later once an EL floor is framed on them.

Building the Floor

Following the same basic sequence for every floor will save time and ease the learning curve.

Layout

The plot plan will give you a starting layout for the joist centers from one side of the structure or occasionally from a starting joist in a measured location. Remember the flange width of your I-joists; for instance, a 2¼-in. flange will need a 1⅛-in. offset to locate the joist centers. Lay out your sills and plates in the usual manner. One of the beauties of

> ### ■ PRO TIP
>
> **As you begin assembling your floor system, pay close attention to the hardware designations on the plot plan. Often there are multiple hangers in your package that are exactly the same size but that have very different load capacities. If you use the wrong one somewhere, you will have a problem in at least one place and probably two.**

> ### ■ PRO TIP
>
> **To snap a bunch of long lines from one end of the house to the other, tie two lines together and wind them back and forth as they need to be rechalked.**

Quick Sequence for Framing a Floor

Here is the sequence that I use for framing a typical floor. Other methods are possible and in some cases may be preferable, but this is usually the most efficient approach.

1. Establish the layout and snap lines across the walls.

2. Locate the openings and frame them with their supporting beams.

3. Install all of the longest joists.

4. Fill in all of the shorter joists.

5. Install the rim joists.

6. Install blocking panels and squash blocks.

7. Install ceiling nailers on the walls below.

8. Subfloor it.

Layout Point

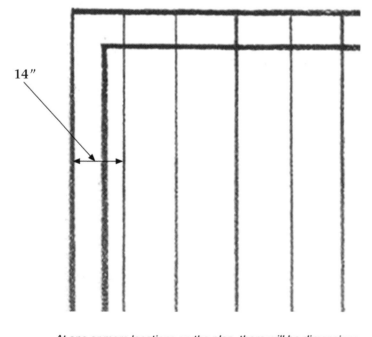

14"

At one or more locations on the plan, there will be dimensions that provide a starting point for the common joist spacing layout. These ensure the structural integrity of the assembled system, as well as clearance for plumbing fixture drain pipes.

EL framing is the long lengths of the stock, so take full advantage of it at this stage. Using a chalkline, snap layout lines across the interior supports from one end of the house to the other. Snapping all of the common layout marks before you start will keep things straighter, save time, and help prevent measuring mistakes later.

Openings

In most cases, I find it easiest to assemble the openings first. These are usually framed with larger and heavier materials, which are easier to lift into place without the joists in the way. Also, many of the joists are in turn carried by these beams, so you need to have them in place first. Locate and install the beams in whichever order is easiest, checking that the opening is positioned correctly in the structure, is parallel to the exterior walls (if it's supposed to be), has sides of equal and correct length, and is square. To check for square, use a framing square and then measure the diagonals to be sure. The joist hangers can be installed before or after lifting the beams. (See p. 67 for the pros and cons of installing hangers first.)

I-joists

I-joists are the main elements in most floors, replacing the 2x10s or 2x12s used in conventional framing. In most ways, they are much easier to use than dimension lumber. Gone are such inconveniences as lapped splices, offset layouts, and butt blocks. Their length and strength allow them to span many structures in continuous lengths. Setting these long joists on upper floors does require a few extra hands, though.

Because I-joists can be nailed down effectively through their flanges, there is no need to install rim joists first the way you do with conventional framing. In

Before there is anything in the way, snap joist layout lines from one end of the house to the other.

Put these big beams up while there's nothing in the way.

It's easier and faster to put the hangers on before the beam is raised.

PRO TIP

Because hangers are so hard to remove, I check openings for square when I make the layout marks for the headers, rather than after they are installed.

By moving in 10 ft. or so from the ends, two people can safely carry this 36-ft. I-joist.

More people are needed to safely set the joist on the second floor without breaking it.

fact, there are advantages to installing the joists first. With no rim joist in the way, the I-joists can be measured and set to a line on the plate, resulting in a straighter perimeter. Some framers cut their I-joists to length right in place, but I've never found this to be easier. If a joist is too long or out of square, it's much easier to trim without a rim joist in the way. Also, long joists are often easier to install if they can be slid beyond the wall without lifting them up. Lastly, the rim joist is easier to install when it can be nailed to the ends of the joists. Of course, anywhere that the rim is framed with heavier material and the joists are attached to it with hangers, you'll need to treat it like an opening and install the rim first.

I like to set the longest joists first, while there is more room to maneuver, and then fill in the smaller joists. This approach also allows me to make a mistake or two in cutting; by ordering a few of the shorter joists combined into longer lengths and working from longest to shortest, I protect myself from ending up with pieces too short to finish the job.

Different manufacturers' rim joist material can vary in thickness; most often it is 1¼ in. When I scribe a line for my joist ends on the plate, I leave an extra ⅛ in. It's much easier later to tap the rim joist out a bit than it is to trim a joist to eliminate a bump in the structure. Incidentally, on a wall that I've braced straight to a string (plumbed and lined), I'll snap that line on the top plate for the joists; on walls that still may need adjustment, I'll scribe the line from the edge of the plate.

The joists that aren't carried in hangers are simply nailed onto the bearing walls through the bottom flanges. Unlike conventional joists, I-joists are stable when attached this way; you can't walk on them, but they won't fall over on

Two nails driven through the flanges into the walls hold the joists securely in place, upright and on layout.

their own, and the flanges don't split when you nail them. Before nailing the joists in place, check any interior walls that haven't been braced to make sure they are plumb.

The joists that go into hangers should be cut about ⅛ in. to ¼ in. short. The gap in the hanger does no harm and has several important benefits. It helps to prevent squeaks, allows for beam assemblies that can't be forced to a consistent thickness, allows for some swelling due to weather and humidity, and allows a margin for those of us who are less than perfect in our measuring and cutting. Joists that are too tight can cause bulges in walls or openings later. As the joists are cut, set them in place and nail off the hangers according to the hanger manufacturer's specification.

In general, I only install I-joist hangers first in places where there is nothing to rest the joist on. Anywhere I can, I set the joist first and then the hanger; it's faster, easier, and more accurate.

Cantilevers

The engineering of joists or beams for cantilevered sections of floor will have been done for you, and the details will be provided in the standard application literature with the joists. The level of reinforcing depends on the size and loading of the cantilever and ranges from no reinforcement to web stiffening material on one or both sides of the joists to doubled joists.

Blocking panels and squash blocks

Most floor systems are engineered without the midspan blocking or bridging that conventional floors require. This speeds the framing process and is much friendlier to the subs. However, the engineered plan will often specify blocking panels in certain areas, typically over bearing walls, at cantilevers, and in the rare instances where noncontinuous joists are butted together. The other application for blocking panels is where

Do Not Toenail the Top Flange

When installing joists in hangers, avoid the temptation to toenail the top flange to secure a joist temporarily or to use a toenail to force a joist into a tight hanger. These toenails are among the leading causes of squeaks in finished floors.

Don't do this! It's going to squeak. And put on your safety glasses while you're at it.

The engineer specified a layer of ¾-in. CDX on each side of these cantilevered joists, as well as the blocking panels. Note the upside-down joists, not necessary with I-joists but a conventional framer's habit.

Blocking Panels Along an Edge

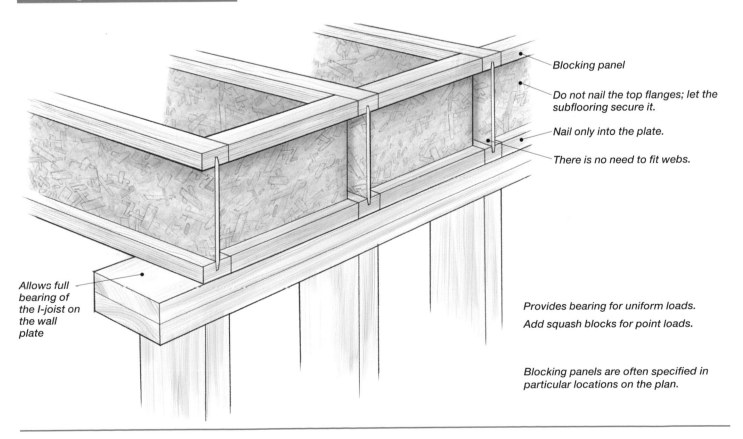

Blocking panel

Do not nail the top flanges; let the subflooring secure it.

Nail only into the plate.

There is no need to fit webs.

Allows full bearing of the I-joist on the wall plate

Provides bearing for uniform loads.

Add squash blocks for point loads.

Blocking panels are often specified in particular locations on the plan.

the joist requires the full width of the plate for bearing surface, and a rim joist can't be used. These blocking panels are simply short sections of I-joist and can usually be cut from scrap or from the extra lengths you bought in case of mistakes (or from your mistakes). Cut them to fit, and secure them by driving toenails in the flanges. There is no need to cut the panels to fit against the webs, just the flanges.

Squash blocks are often neglected but are important elements in the floor system. I-joists are engineered to resist the normal loads of floors and walls

above, but they do not have the compressive strength to handle point loads from the upper floors. These point loads include ridge posts and other structural columns, as well as the jack loads from headers spanning interior and exterior openings. The plot plan will specify locations for squash blocks to transfer these loads through the floor system to the bearing structure below. Sometimes there will be an entire row of squash blocks where a bearing wall sits above and perpendicular to the joists. These blocks are typically cut from 2x4 or 2x6 material, $\frac{1}{16}$ in. longer than the nominal joist size. They are nailed to the flanges alongside the joists.

Rim joists

Depending on the configuration of the building and the load on the perimeter walls, the plan will be specific in its requirements for the edge of the floor. Most often, the requirement is for rim joist material, which is usually 1¼-in. LSL or LVL material that matches the joist depth. Occasionally, more load capacity will be required, and the rim joist will be doubled or replaced with heavier material. In addition, you might have selected a stronger material, such as an LVL, to carry the attachment of a porch or deck ledger.

When the I-joists are all installed, it's fast and easy to go around and nail on the rim joist. Just use full lengths wherever possible, and fill in to the corners. You can make the butt joints anywhere—they don't even need to be on joists, although most carpenters do it that way.

There are specific fastening requirements for rim joists, both to the plates or sills and to the joists. A typical nailing schedule would have 12d nails at a 6-in. spacing into the plate and two 12d nails into each joist flange.

These squash blocks are made from 2x6 stock and carry corner loads. The hammer holds them in place while the nailer secures them. The metal rods are anchor-bolt extensions, which will secure hold-down hardware.

PRO TIP

Because you need to start a subfloor with a rip anyway, check the measurements for large openings or wings, and plan for efficient use of time and material cutoffs.

The rim joist is back-nailed on after the joists are set. Putting this many toenails into a 2x10 rim joist would split the bottom of it right off.

Unlike on conventionally framed floors, the subflooring on an EL floor needs to be trimmed flush and nailed thoroughly.

Subflooring

After the floor is framed and nailed off and all of the miscellaneous pieces are in place, it can be subfloored. This process is not much different than for a conventional floor: Snap a starting line for the first course of plywood, apply glue, and nail or screw down the subflooring. One significant difference is that the edge of the plywood needs to have the groove ripped off and needs to fully contact the rim joist, unlike a conventional floor where the subfloor can and should be held back ¼ in. (My building inspector tells me that this is a common mistake, and there is no good fix other than adding blocking underneath.)

CHAPTER 8

Engineered Components in Wall Framing

HE ADVENT OF ENGINEERED materials hasn't much changed the design and construction of walls, but it has provided some helpful new options. Of course, stronger materials allow thinner walls to resist greater loads, but I've found the biggest advantage is that EL keeps things straight. Like every other framer, I've spent a good part of my time culling through piles of stock looking for straight plates and studs; EL pretty much eliminates the bother.

LSL or TimberStrand

LSL stock in nominal 2x4 and 2x6 sizes was developed by the TrusJoist Company as their TimberStrand® Frameworks® system. The same LSL stock is used for both studs and plates, although PSL columns might be incorporated. The original intent was to develop a wall-framing system capable of withstanding the loads typically required of taller walls, without incorporating extra engineered elements such as steel bracing. The system works well for this application, allowing the construction of walls up to 22 ft. tall without intermediate platforms. Framers quickly discovered this material and began using it for other applications, most notably for plate stock and for gable end framing. The advantages of having a pile of perfectly straight 2x6 material 24 ft. long when laying out wall plates are obvious: no culling, fewer splices, and straighter walls.

The dimensional stability of LSL wall-framing material is an advantage as well. Because the plate stock doesn't split when nailed near the ends, the bulges that so often show through wall finishes are eliminated and the intersecting corners of the walls go together more tightly. Another prime application for these plates is in framing gable ends. Even a modest-size house may require gable plates of 20 ft. or longer; framing these with one piece rather than splicing two or more pieces is faster and creates a straighter wall.

LSL studs are a joy, too. They eliminate culling and crowning, and their dimensional consistency puts an end to those thick spots around window and door openings. Specific framing details that require stability and precision, such as interior cabinetry soffits, are also good applications. It may be that LSL studs don't hold nails and screws as well as sawn lumber, although I've never seen any evidence of this. Of course, they don't split either, and their edges are never missing. In any case, things that need secure fastening to walls, such as cabinetry and handrails, should be attached to wooden blocking.

The 22-ft.-long LSL wall plates are perfectly straight and eliminate the need for many splices in long walls.

■ PRO TIP

It's OK to use LSL for plates and sawn lumber for studs in the same wall. I don't use a mix of LSL and sawn lumber for plates in the same wall, though. The slight differences in stability may be enough to affect the structure later.

Why don't we frame entire houses with this stuff? I'd love to, but at this time, the board-foot price is more than double that for sawn lumber. I use it where it saves enough time or where the improved results justify the extra cost. There is no problem with using a hybrid approach in most wall framing; Trus Joist calls this "Zone Framing." A typically cost-effective approach today uses EL plates and headers and conventional or finger-jointed studs.

Finger-Jointed Studs

Finger-jointed studs are made from short pieces of sawn lumber, often scrap, glued together end to end. The better ones are dressed after assembly to a smooth and consistent finish, so they're a pleasure to handle and use. They've been around for a long time and are the next best thing to LSL studs in terms of fast, straight framing. That is, if they are of good quality;

LSL is used for the plates, ridge post, and king studs of this gable wall.

These 24-ft. LSL fly rafters will make for straight rake trim.

▪ PRO TIP

If you're in the habit of buying a few long pieces of sawn lumber for specific applications, such as 2x4s or 2x6s more than 20 ft. long, check the price. Suppliers often charge a premium for this material; the cost of LSL stock may not be much more.

I've had some delivered that were poorly made and no straighter than very bad sawn lumber. Watch for misaligned joints, irregular dimensions, excessive wane or bark, large knots, and bends. Generally though, they are of much better quality and are less expensive than sawn lumber.

Wall Headers

Criteria for a good wall header include:

- ▪ It should be strong enough to carry the load.

- ▪ Its thickness should match or fit within the thickness of the wall.

- ▪ Its depth should fit over the opening.

Also, a header needs to resist short-term shrinkage and long-term settlement, and it should not swell up and bulge under the trim around the opening. It needs to be economical and easy to install, too. If it is light enough to lift, has some insulation value, and has a place to run wires, those are all nice bonuses. Small wonder then that most of the time spent on building walls involves the headers.

EL provides some excellent options for wall headers. See the chart on p. 87 for the pros and cons of various options.

Prefabricated header stock

Several manufacturers make engineered header material, usually composed of a top and bottom flange of sawn lumber, connected by two OSB or plywood webs, and filled with foam insulation. This material is available in various depths and thicknesses to fit different wall-framing applications. Like other EL products, headers cut from this stock are lighter, straighter, and stronger than the usual assemblies of sawn lumber. They also are perfectly consistent in dimension, so you

Manufactured headers are great time-savers, but they have their limitations.

can precut trimmers instead of fitting them individually as you often need to do with other header materials. I began using them years ago when they first became available, and I've determined that they are almost always cost effective; however, they do have some significant drawbacks (see p. 87).

Site-built I-joist headers

Headers assembled on site from I-joists are not a prescribed use of this material, but they have some advantages. Like prefab headers, they will only span short openings with no point loads. They take a bit longer to assemble, and they aren't insulated. However, by building them with the flanges flush to the outside of the wall, they provide good nailing surfaces for trim. Also, the greater depth of the webs gives the electrician an easy path

LVL headers were ripped to fit trimmed openings in bearing walls.

over the openings, too. Lastly, they are an efficient use of short leftover material.

Other header options

Because prefab headers are limited in their load-bearing capabilities, many walls utilize other forms of EL headers. The choices for these headers are the same as for beams and girders: LVL, LSL, or PSL.

LVLs are strong and versatile. At 1¾ in. thick, two of them fit perfectly in a 2x4 wall, while three fit in a 2x6 wall with a strip of ¼-in. material added for nailing thickness. They are especially good for arched headers because they are available in depths up to 18 in., and the curved cut can be done in several layers rather than in one large piece. A circular saw will cut a

This LSL header spans a door in a bearing wall.

fairly tight curve in 1¾-in. material, so cutting the curve in the header one layer at a time is much easier than cutting the same curve in thicker material.

LSL and PSL headers are occasionally specified and are used just as solid timber headers. In the correct dimension, both will provide solid nailing on both sides of the wall. LSL is more economical than LVL; PSL is slightly stronger. The choice is generally made by the engineer or designer.

Interior wall headers

Interior wall headers have the same criteria as exterior headers, except that they don't need insulation value and are typically in 2x4 walls, rather than 2x6. The old standard bearing header—two 2xs with a plywood spacer—still works; in fact, ⅞₆-in. OSB works better than ½-in. CDX. However, EL headers made of LSL or LVL are much better in every way but material cost.

Columns in Walls

The advent of heavily engineered structures with wide-open spaces and specified load paths has resulted in a need for columns that fit within walls. Before EL, we used solid timber, multiple studs nailed together, or integrated steel columns in our walls. We still use all of these methods, but more often now we can use a single PSL column. These columns can carry greater loads within a smaller wall, stay straighter and more uniform in thickness, and are faster to install.

One new development is the LSL 45-degree corner column. Available in pairs, they are nailed together to create a perfect 45-degree corner in a wall or angled bay. Since the loads on these bays

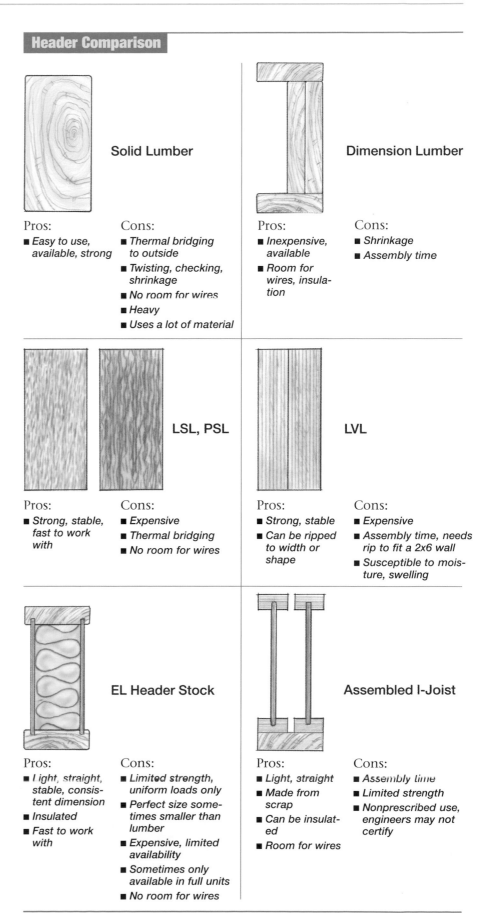

Header Comparison

Solid Lumber

Pros:
- Easy to use, available, strong

Cons:
- Thermal bridging to outside
- Twisting, checking, shrinkage
- No room for wires
- Heavy
- Uses a lot of material

Dimension Lumber

Pros:
- Inexpensive, available
- Room for wires, insulation

Cons:
- Shrinkage
- Assembly time

LSL, PSL

Pros:
- Strong, stable, fast to work with

Cons:
- Expensive
- Thermal bridging
- No room for wires

LVL

Pros:
- Strong, stable
- Can be ripped to width or shape

Cons:
- Expensive
- Assembly time, needs rip to fit a 2x6 wall
- Susceptible to moisture, swelling

EL Header Stock

Pros:
- Light, straight, stable, consistent dimension
- Insulated
- Fast to work with

Cons:
- Limited strength, uniform loads only
- Perfect size sometimes smaller than lumber
- Expensive, limited availability
- Sometimes only available in full units
- No room for wires

Assembled I-Joist

Pros:
- Light, straight
- Made from scrap
- Can be insulated
- Room for wires

Cons:
- Assembly time
- Limited strength
- Nonprescribed use, engineers may not certify

A 5¼-in. square PSL column fits into a 2x6 wall and carries the load from the ridge above to a beam below.

Note that the column doesn't bear on the plate or subfloor but goes through to the beam below.

usually are not great, the corner posts can be combined with 1x4 trimmers to make a compact assembly. Forty-five-degree corners in interior walls are also easy with this product. They are a great time-saver that make a strong, straight corner with good nailing inside and out.

OSB Wall Sheathing

OSB is rapidly replacing plywood as the structural wall sheathing of choice. This is probably because of its lower cost, but OSB has other advantages, too. It's flat,

Spreading the Load with Steel Plates

As you use high-strength columns, watch the bearing strength of the materials that they rest on. If an engineered PSL column is built into a wall with three spruce 2x4 bottom plates, the plates will likely compress. An effective and easy way to address this is by adding short steel plates over and under the column to spread the compressive loads to a longer section of the wall plates.

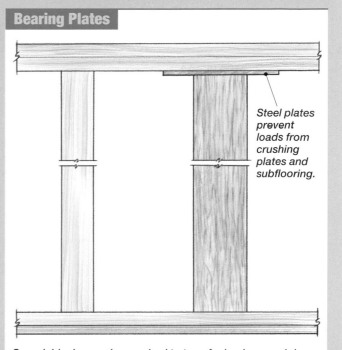

Bearing Plates

Steel plates prevent loads from crushing plates and subflooring.

Squash blocks may be required to transfer loads up and down grain perpendicular to loads area similar to plates.

Consult an engineer if in doubt.

For an alternative method, see the photo on the facing page.

stable, and not subject to the voids, delamination, and warping that plywood is prone to. It has a slick side and a textured side that is easy to walk on, but it isn't critical that it be used right-side out. Best of all, it has lines marked on it in both directions at 16 in. and 24 in. o.c. These lines are a great help in aligning studs, rafters, and trusses and when nailing it off. You can even use them as cut lines. OSB does have some disadvantages. It tends to swell up when it gets wet, especially along cut edges. This can wreak havoc with extension jambs, doors, and other trim. Also, although it has the same strength rating as ½-in. plywood, most carpenters would agree that it's a bit weaker, especially on a roof built with rafters 24 in. o.c.

This angled bay uses LSL 45-degree corner posts and 1x4 trimmers. The result is fast and easy assembly and minimal trim between the windows.

CHAPTER 9

Framing Roofs

This roof, framed with I-joist rafters, is perfectly flat and straight.

A LTHOUGH ENGINEERED framing systems were first developed for floors, many of their benefits are equally applicable to building roofs. The limitations of sawn lumber, such as crown and twist, shrinkage, and instability, still apply. In comparison, I-joists are almost perfectly straight, and they can support spans of just about any length that you might find in residential construction. And since rafters need to be lifted high into place with person power, it is a great advantage to use lightweight I-joists.

There are some drawbacks to EL roof systems, though, and so while engineered floors are revolutionizing the framing business, engineered roofs are not yet prevalent. I've built roofs using materials and designs from some of the leading manufacturers in the industry, and at this time, all of them are using imperfect adaptations of design software that was originally developed for floors. Engineered roof systems are hardware intensive, which makes for strong, wind-resistant structures but which also makes for a slower and more labor-intensive assembly process. Also, some of the more complex hardware applications are either unavailable or need to be custom made.

In addition, engineered roof systems almost universally incorporate structural ridge beams, which introduce design considerations affecting the lower levels and exterior of the structure. Not only does this affect the design of the gable ends but also dictates interior columns that you might not find with other types of construction.

Since the primary benefits of engineered systems—flatness, stability, and strength—are less critical in roofs than in floors, the added costs are harder to justify. At the time of this writing, my feeling is that only simple gable roofs are approaching the break-even point in cost/benefit ratio. However, this is changing as these systems evolve. And after all, it's not such a bad thing to spend a bit more to build a better structure.

Engineered Roof Design

As with floors, the initial design for an engineered roof will be generated by the materials manufacturer when you enter your plans and design parameters into their proprietary software system. The software systems that I've seen are based on floor-framing software, adapted to incorporate the loading and length

■ **PRO TIP**

If you're a professional builder and have some control over the design and materials used in your projects, don't build an EL roof until you've done some EL floors. Then, start with a basic gable roof with minimal complications. This will ease the learning process and probably save you time and money.

Roof Plot Plan

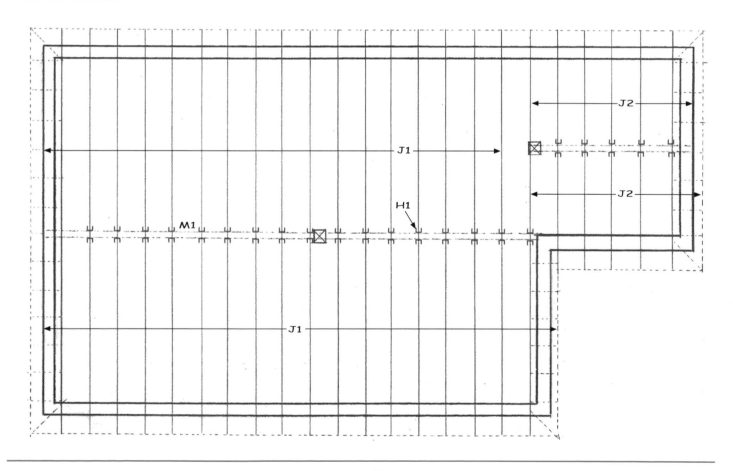

Roof Headers

Headers in Roof Structures

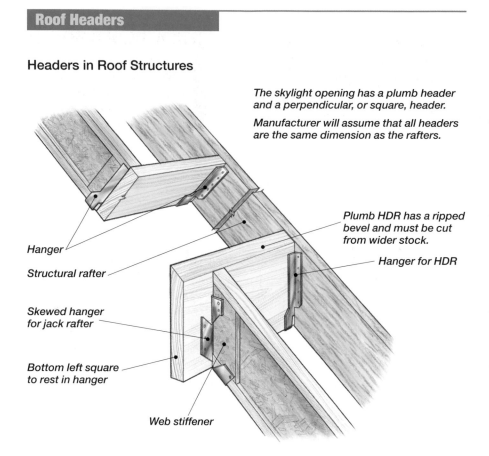

The skylight opening has a plumb header and a perpendicular, or square, header.

Manufacturer will assume that all headers are the same dimension as the rafters.

Hanger

Structural rafter

Skewed hanger for jack rafter

Bottom left square to rest in hanger

Web stiffener

Plumb HDR has a ripped bevel and must be cut from wider stock.

Hanger for HDR

A skylight opening often has both a plumb header and a perpendicular header, like this, as opposed to a chimney opening that has only plumb headers. A dormer header will be plumb and will often be beveled to match the main roof pitch.

A Double Header to Carry a Dormer Ridge and Valleys

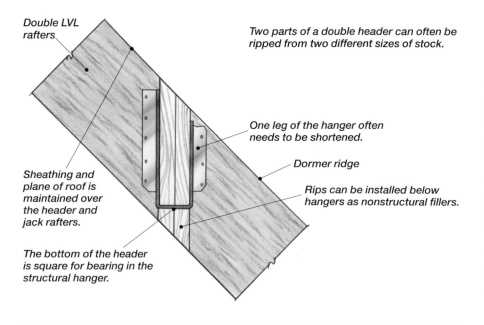

Double LVL rafters

Two parts of a double header can often be ripped from two different sizes of stock.

Sheathing and plane of roof is maintained over the header and jack rafters.

One leg of the hanger often needs to be shortened.

Dormer ridge

Rips can be installed below hangers as nonstructural fillers.

The bottom of the header is square for bearing in the structural hanger.

changes introduced by slope. With these systems still in their technological youth, careful checking is required before ordering a roof-framing package.

Structural ridges

There are several things to check here. First, if the entire structure was designed for engineered framing, the point loads for ridge posts should be addressed at each level, starting in the basement. These posts may be at intermediate points as well as at the gable ends. Check to make sure that they all line up vertically and that they belong in the floor plan, either as exposed columns or in walls. If headers are used to transfer the loads laterally, make sure that they fit into the walls and over the openings. Next, make sure that you can actually get the ridge to where it needs to go. Most designs will use a built-up ridge of multiple LVLs, sometimes spliced over the posts but often in full-length pieces as long as 44 ft. Sometimes a ridge will be specified as a single larger member, such as an LSL. With ridge heights often 30 ft. or more up in the air, you need to look at the size of the ridge and the size of your crew and figure out how to get it safely up there.

Openings

All of the software that I've seen to date treats roofs like floors and assumes openings with headers framed square to the rafters, rather than plumb (vertical) or flat (horizontal). This works for some openings but not for all. Structurally, it can work to your advantage to orient the headers so they are plumb; doing so allows you to install deeper headers. The better programs (or engineers) have figured out that dormer headers are plumb, although they don't always calculate the depth correctly.

Hips and valleys

The same issue with material depth applies here as well. Just as with conventional framing, a hip or valley rafter typically needs to be at least one size larger than the rafters, for instance, an 11⅞-in. LVL valley with 9½-in. I-joist rafters. You also need to check the lengths of these members carefully; the better software operators will have it figured out correctly, but don't depend on it. Lastly, modern engineering practice assumes that hips and valleys are fully load bearing and need to be structurally supported at the ends.

Hardware

Many of the connections in a roof structure will be made with adjustable hangers that can be both sloped and skewed, such as Simpson LSSUI35s. However, there are several other hardware issues to check. Some connections will be made with a special-order hanger, which is factory built to a specific slope and/or skew condition and must be ordered as much as four to six weeks ahead of time. Some connections are listed as "not found," which means that some creative solution is called for. Also, when you adjust the depths of headers around openings and

The versatile LSSUI hanger can be installed sloped up, sloped down, square, or skewed and sloped.

PRO TIP

The manufacturer's plot plan will often neglect to include rafters on the gables; be sure you add them to the count.

at intersection ridges, you often need to adjust the size of the hangers accordingly. See chapter 3 for more information on EL hardware.

Roofs You Can't or Shouldn't Build with EL

At this stage in its evolution, EL lends itself well to straightforward gable roof designs. It can be adapted well to other designs such as simple hip roofs, and it can be forced into framing almost anything. But look carefully at the cost/benefit ratio before deciding to use EL.

Some roof structures are virtually impossible to build with EL at this time. These include most curved structures, as well as irregular valleys that require skewed connections more acute than 45 degrees. Hybrid approaches are common, and because differential shrinkage is not a problem in roof construction, they are perfectly acceptable. Engineers and builders have been substituting engineered structural components such as ridges and valleys into conventional roofs for many years. Sometimes a designer will recommend that conventional framing be incorporated for the more complex elements of an EL roof; this is a practical and effective approach.

Assembling the Engineered Roof

Framing a typical roof with engineered materials is essentially the same as framing one with conventional lumber. The only real differences are in the specific techniques for assembling the components. As with any other framing process,

there is more than one right way; I'll focus on the methods that have worked for me.

Laying out the roof and raising the gables

Use conventional framing techniques for laying out the roof, rafters, and gables. I use standard rise/run formulas to determine ridge heights and gable end layout, and I create a pattern rafter using whatever stock my rafters will be made of. Gable ends can be built and stood prior to raising the roof, or they can be framed in afterward. I frame and sheath mine first, incorporating ridge posts of the correct height and leaving a generous pocket in which to set my ridge beams. Then I stand each end up, check for plumb, and temporarily brace.

Alternately, rim joist material could be used, but I-joists are lighter, straighter, less expensive, and strong enough. Some houses with wide overhangs may require an alternate approach with cantilevered lookouts built from sawn lumber. The engineer will determine this and provide a detail.

The pattern rafter

The concept of making and using a pattern rafter with EL is the same as many of us use in conventional framing. I make my pattern rafter when I have the gable ends laid out on the floor; I make one, test it for fit, and then make four more. I use those four on the gable walls, and keep the first for roof framing. When the ridge is up, I test it again, checking and adjusting as needed for the flange thickness of the hangers. I then use it as a pattern for the rest of the common rafters. Of course, other framers have their own methods, which might differ from mine.

This gable end has its I-joist rafters in place against a ridge post, creating a pocket for the structural ridge.

Raising the ridge

Most main ridges are built with multiple LVLs, often two or three 1¾-in. by 14-in. members, depending on the size of the roof and the span between intermediate supports. Like carrying beams, these LVLs are cut to length, lifted into position one at a time, and spiked together. EL ridges will generally support their own weight without deflection, so I set them up and put the intermediate posts in place under them. Then I set up a taut line and brace the posts to hold the ridge straight.

The ridge is raised into place one ply at a time.

The ridge posts are installed and plumbed as the ridge is braced straight.

Structural rafters

Dormers, bays, skylights, chimney holes, and other openings are flanked by structural rafters that are made from LVLs, multiple LVLs, LSLs, or occasionally PSLs. Sometimes doubled or tripled I-joists are used; I cut these along with the rest of the common rafters. Using the pattern rafter, I cut and set the structural rafters first, attaching them with the hangers specified on the plot plan and carefully keeping the ridge straight. Built-up LVLs and other heavy-duty ridges are fairly stiff, so keeping them straight really just means not forcing them out of line with the first few rafters. I keep a string set up above the ridge just to be sure.

Common rafters

Most of the roof is framed with I-joists, which replace the 2x material normally used for rafters. Because I-joists are straight and stand nicely on edge, it's easy to gang-cut all of the rafters at once.

The structural rafters are installed using the specified hardware.

Web Stiffeners

Web stiffeners are small blocks of solid material added to the sides of I-joists to connect the flanges and transfer loads. They also serve as attachment surfaces for hardware connectors and as additional bearing surface in some applications. They are only occasionally specified in floor systems but are generally required for roof rafters.

Because of the variety of sizes and shapes necessary, manufacturers specify them but won't supply them; you need to make them up in the field. They need to be sized to fill the thickness between the edge of the flange and the web. I-joists with 3½-in. flanges and ½-in. webs, such as TJI-Pro 550s, can use solid 2x material for web stiffeners, provided the grain is oriented to carry compressive loads. More often, the web stiffener needs to be fabricated from some other material. For the TJI-Pro 130s that we used throughout this house, the required thickness is ⅞ in. We made this by gluing two sheets of ⁷⁄₁₆-in. OSB together with exterior-grade yellow glue. The resulting material was cut into angled web stiffeners for the 10-pitch roof using a tablesaw and slide saw.

For this house, we'll glue up five pairs of sheets. With OSB, be sure to glue the non-slick surfaces.

A slide saw with a stop is best for cutting the stiffeners.

A big tablesaw makes this job easier and safer.

■ PRO TIP

Rip the web stiffener stock to the web width first. The length doesn't need to be precise. Also, this will allow you to save a few longer pieces for making templates and jigs and for backing hangers.

■ PRO TIP

Don't let your finished web stiffeners get wet; they will swell up, making hardware installation much more difficult.

■ PRO TIP

The stock you rip for making web stiffeners has a variety of other uses:

- It's a good base for marking and cutting jigs.
- It fills I-joists where you need nailing, either for hardware or for finish materials.
- It is required when fastening several I-joists together.
- You can splice a joist in a nonstructural application such as on a gable or dormer cheek.

PRO TIP

When measuring lengths of rafters, allow for the thickness of the hanger at one or both ends. This averages about 3/16 in. per end, depending on the type of hanger.

The rafter preparation is repetitive, so I set up an assembly sequence. For general instructions on cutting I-joists, see p. 52.

1. Stack the rafters tightly together on the deck, top edge down, and mark them using the pattern rafter and a chalk-line. The bottom flange can be cut for the plumb cut, bird's mouth, and heel.

2. Lift the rafters to a cutting station and finish the cuts at both ends. Because the web cuts don't matter, I overcut them a bit by eye, but if you prefer, you can make a marking jig and cut them exactly.

Rafters for the entire roof are stacked and gang-cut. The pattern rafter in the foreground was used to test the fit in the roof and then to mark the stacked rafters from both sides.

The cuts are finished one at a time as the rafters are taken from the stack.

A simple jig helps make the marks across the webs, especially on wider joists.

3. Install the web stiffeners. Nail them in from both sides according to the manufacturer's fastening schedule.

4. Install the hangers. After all of the rafters are cut, assembled, and prepped, I set them in place like any other common rafters, holding the tops slightly high until the bird's mouths are nailed, then fastening the top hanger to the ridge. This part of the process is fast and fun.

Headers and holes

With the structural and common rafters in place, I set headers for dormers, bays, and openings. If the headers are to be set plumb, rip the tops to a bevel that matches the roof slope, but leave the bottoms square to set in hangers. If the interior ceiling is to be finished, make sure the header doesn't project below the plane of the rafters; if the ceiling will not be finished, it doesn't matter. Generally, I tack the headers in place with spikes and

Web stiffeners are installed as required.

The hangers are installed.

The completed rafters are lifted and nailed in place.

The header is tacked in place...

...and the hanger is fitted afterward.

then fit the hangers; sometimes, for a very heavy header, I set the hangers first and drop the header into them (see p. 99). Occasionally, I'll mount the hangers on the ends of a short header and nail it into position that way. There is no one correct method—do whatever is easier in the situation.

After the headers are in place—and, in some cases, after the hips or valleys are set (see below)—I fill in the jack rafters around them. Jack rafters are prepped the same way as common rafters, except that there is a hanger for each end.

Hips and valleys

Hip and valley rafters are laid out, cut, and fitted just as for a conventional frame. Plot plans often specify hangers for the ends of these members that are "not found," which means that they are not standard items or are not available at all. Sometimes I adapt another hanger, a universal connector, or a length of steel strap; sometimes I resort to the time-honored method of toenailing. For some high-load situations, the engineer may require a custom-made piece of hardware. None of this is any different from the issues faced in assembling a conventional frame.

What is different is the jack rafters that go in after the hips or valleys are set. I've been on production sites where these jack rafters were cut square and side-nailed, but in the custom framing world, standard practice is to use compound-miter cuts. With I-joists, there are no compound miters; they are assembled with skewable hangers that fit on square plumb cuts.

The jack rafters are cut, prepped, and installed. The hanger should be bent only once, so do it right in place.

There is no easy way to nail the inside of these skewed hangers. Some people recommend nailing them first and then bending the rafter into position, but I've never been able to make it work accurately. Sometimes I nail them using a drift punch.

■ **PRO TIP**

Some hip and valley hardware does require that you alter the normal sequence that you are probably accustomed to. There is a discussion of this on pp. 26–27 .

Standard Lumber for Fill-In

There comes a point where it makes more sense to cut a short jack rafter out of a 2x6, since its only purpose is to support a small span of sheathing.

There's no point cutting and prepping an I-joist this short; just use a scrap of 2x material.

Overhangs, blocking, and trim backing

There are limits to the allowable overhangs that I-joist rafters can support, both at the eaves and on the gables. The manufacturer's literature will offer various options for framing or strengthening overhangs. I generally use a structural subfascia ripped from 2x material, which is attached to the cut-off top flanges and to soffit blocking underneath.

Many EL roofs are designed with rafters 24 in. o.c., which saves time and material but requires special consideration for the roof sheathing. In some areas, ½-in. sheathing can be used with H-clips to protect the unsupported edges. In others, depending on codes, engineering, and wind loading, solid blocking is required on all sheathing edges. I cut these blocks from scrap 2x4 material and toenail them in along snapped lines.

Eave detail for a typical house. Notice that the attic floor joists are perpendicular to the rafters.

Rafter Tail

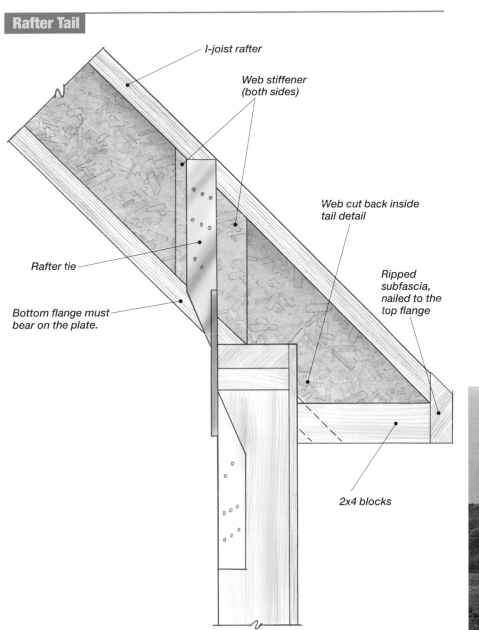

I-joist rafter

Web stiffener
(both sides)

Web cut back inside
tail detail

Rafter tie

Ripped
subfascia,
nailed to the
top flange

Bottom flange must
bear on the plate.

2x4 blocks

The details at the eaves will depend on the size of the overhang, as well as on the types of material, hardware, and trim used. This is a typical Cape or Colonial type of eave detail.

■ PRO TIP

The hardest part of hip and valley framing with I-joists is overcoming the lifetime habit of using "long point" measurements for layout and length. With skewed hangers, both layout and length are measured at what would be the "short point" on a conventional compound cut. I wish I could say there was a trick for breaking this habit.

Perimeter blocking for the edges of the roof sheathing is required by some codes.

A combination of USP RT-20s and SST H6s holds these rafters down.
The exact configuration depends on what is below the rafter.

Hardware to hold it together

All building codes now require some sort of rafter tie-down hardware. I use a combination of types of hardware, depending on the load and configuration. The other component usually specified is a rafter tie over the ridge, particularly on steep slope applications, which most manufacturers consider to be greater than 4/12. These can be purchased but are more often cut from steel strap material, sized, and fastened according to the manufacturer's specifications (see p. 28).

Cover It Up!

Sheathing an EL roof is a pleasure. The flanges are wide, 24 in. o.c. makes for faster nailing, and when it's finished there are no unsightly bulges from excessively crowned rafters. There are only two things that worry me. One is getting my new EL structure weatherproof as soon as possible. The other is that I may stay in business long enough to have to take one of these things apart in a remodeling project someday.

The ridge straps are installed.

CHAPTER 10

Trusses

TRUSSES ARE ASSEMBLIES OF wood and steel components configured in a way that maximizes efficiency. By analyzing the structural requirements of a given building task, such as supporting a floor, ceiling, roof, or bridge, a truss can be designed to do the job using less material than any conventionally framed system. Trusses, like I-joists, make use of the excellent tensile and compressive properties of wood fiber and are generally assembled using the connective properties of steel.

There are trusses for almost any floor or roof design you can imagine and for some you can't. The types of trusses available, their design, their applications, and the techniques for installing them could fill an entire book on their own. In this chapter, I'll give a brief overview of trusses and how they fit into the world of residential framing.

Types of Trusses

Trusses can be classified by their application, shape, or the way they are constructed. Trusses designed for floor systems or for flat roofs are known as bar trusses, floor trusses, or parallel chord trusses. They are, as their names imply, flat or nearly so. Roof trusses are designed to create the shape of the roof, whether it's a simple gable or something more complex such as a gambrel, hip roof, or a mansard. Roof trusses also can be designed to create interior spaces; for instance, a set of scissor trusses can form a cathedral ceiling. Exotic trusses can be designed and built to create almost any roof and ceiling configuration.

For large-scale applications where the size of the supporting structure is not limited, trusses can offer a wide range of solutions. Big, open-plan buildings and bridges are good examples. Some structures, such as pedestrian walkways, are even built within trussed frames.

Most floor or bar trusses are sold and purchased as standard items. Truss manufacturers provide tables that you can consult to determine span, depth, and design strength. They are not off-the-shelf items that you can buy at your local home center, but most lumberyards have access to a supplier. Larger trusses are awkward to transport on a standard delivery truck, so the supplier will deliver them directly using a specialized vehicle or trailer.

Roof trusses are occasionally site built, using sawn lumber and nailed-on connection plates or plywood gussets. Most building officials today will require that an engineer design, detail, and perhaps certify these site-built trusses, so this is not generally a cost-effective option. Many roof trusses are mass-produced in standard shapes and sizes by manufacturers who target the production framing market. They also can be custom designed and built.

General Types of Roof Trusses

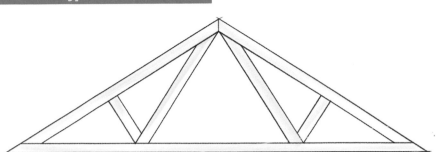

Simple gable truss

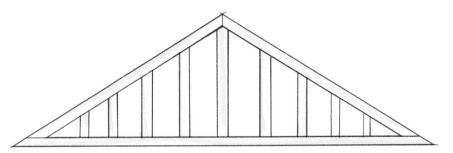

Gable end truss

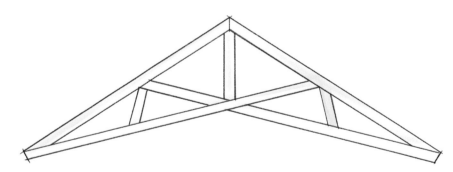

Scissor truss

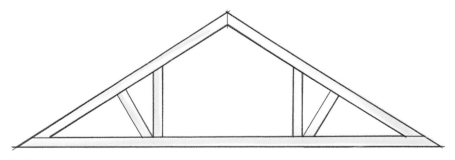

Attic truss

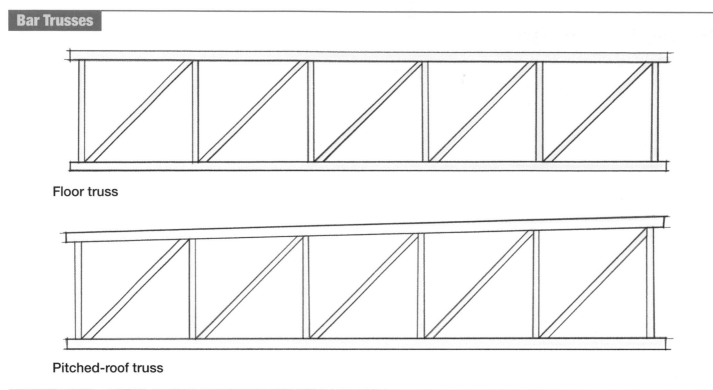

Floor truss

Pitched-roof truss

Disadvantages of Trusses

Trusses have their downsides, both as floor and roof systems. Many jobs are not appropriate for them.

A house built with a trussed roof has no attic space to speak of, although there are trusses that incorporate a small attic area. You can crawl through the webs to run wires and pipes, but space is limited and it's not fun.

A small framing crew can handle trusses up to about 24 ft. by hand, but for anything larger, you are dependent on a crane for delivery and installation. This introduces complications in scheduling, weather, and site logistics.

Trusses, especially large roof trusses, can be dangerous. When I was a young carpenter, I let a set of 60-ft. trusses on a utility building collapse. As they went

down like dominoes, only luck saved the crew from serious injury.

In many jurisdictions, buildings constructed with trusses are considered hazardous to firefighters and to the occupants of the building in the event of a fire. This is because trusses tend to cause floors and roofs to collapse catastrophically after relatively minor damage to the tensile bottom chords. Special labeling and sometimes extra fireproofing are required.

Lastly, trusses can be a real problem when it comes time to remodel the building. Even something as simple as a skylight can require serious reengineering; dormers, lofts, cathedral ceilings, and other popular remodels are close to impossible.

Applications for Parallel Chord Trusses

Parallel chord trusses, or bar trusses, can be made entirely of wood or can be a combination of wood and steel. They were fairly popular about 20 years ago, primarily as an efficient way to build a clear span floor or ceiling of 24 ft. or more. In my opinion, they have been made largely obsolete by the advent of high-strength wood I-joists, which can handle most of those applications today.

However, because they are so strong, there are still places where trusses can be a better solution. One is for creating clear spans more than 32 ft. or so or for clear spans where lack of deflection (bounce or springiness) is a high priority. Another is in structures where floor-system depth is not restricted and where a lot of room is needed to run utilities such as high-volume ductwork. The web openings in many bar trusses are big enough for large ducts to pass through with no cutting or drilling; they can even be custom designed with space to meet a particular ducting requirement. Roof systems in flat-roofed structures also are a good application for bar trusses, especially if they are designed with the roof pitch built in. All of these applications are more prevalent in commercial construction than in residential work.

There is another feature of parallel chord trusses that can make them the right choice for certain applications. In many cases, the top or bottom chords can carry the truss independently. This allows the trusses to be hung down from their supporting wall or ledger. It also allows the top chord to be cut back for roof clearance in a way that cannot be done with I-joists.

Bar Truss Details

Top-Chord Supported Floor Truss
This system can bring the floor level down close to grade.

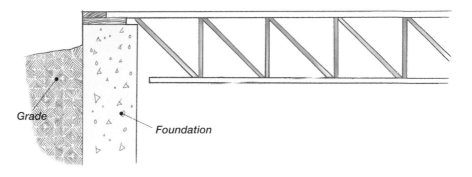

Grade

Foundation

Bottom-Chord Supported Truss
An I-joist cannot be cut like this. This allows a much lower eave height.

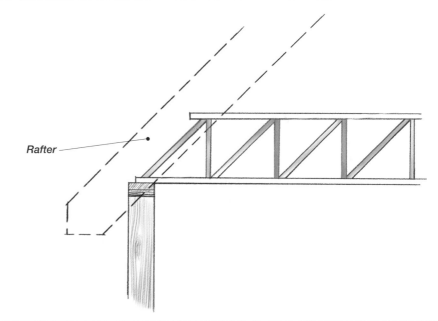

Rafter

■ PRO

If you are going to run ducts, make sure the trusses are all aligned from the same end. Otherwise, the web locations may not match from one to the next.

Roof Trusses

Simple gable-roof trusses are a mainstay of the production housing market and are installed on tens of thousands of ranch-style homes every year, as well as on garages, additions, and commercial and agricultural buildings. Their chief advantages are economy, speed of construction, and flexibility in the interior. They are available generally in 2-ft. increments in lengths from 16 ft. to more than 60 ft. and in a variety of shapes. The tricks for installing them safely and efficiently could fill a book, and even finishing a house built with them is different from other types of construction. More exotic trussed roofs, like EL systems, are usually designed, engineered, and sold as packages. These packages can create just about any roof and in many cases are faster and less expensive than the equivalent stick-framing process. They are certainly faster and more efficient than an EL system for almost any roof, at least at this time.

Engineers and builders who use roof trusses extensively have made a science of efficient design and construction. Complex roofs can be built in the factory, assembled on site at ground level, and lifted into place using a crane.

This roof is being assembled with a custom-built set of trusses.

The entire hipped end of this roof was assembled on the ground and is being lifted into place.

A pile of simple gable trusses is ready to go up. Instant roof!

Subcontractors and the Engineered Structure

TALKING ABOUT SUBCONTRAC-TORS in chapter 11 seems appropriate, since they so often end up in bankruptcy proceedings! This is usually from buying $40,000 pickup trucks, but their troubles can often be your troubles too, especially if they mess up your engineered building. This chapter will help you manage your subs so your project proceeds smoothly and the structure remains strong.

A building framed with engineered material needs to be seen as a complete package, rather than as an assemblage of independent components. The primary benefit of this approach is structural efficiency. Each piece, with its associated hardware and labor, is fully utilized; unnecessary labor and material are eliminated. Just as the building frame is considered as a whole, the rest of the project should be looked at in the same way. This is not different from conventional construction, it's just much more important when using EL.

Educating the Subs

There is a learning process for the framers when switching from conventional framing to EL. The same applies to the subcontractors who follow the framers. EL provides substantial benefits to the subs, especially to those whose work depends on strength, straightness, and stability. However, there also are substantial potential liabilities in an EL system: A careless or uneducated subcontractor can destroy an engineered structural system in short order. In fact, my building official cites this as the single biggest issue he has with EL construction.

It's the GC's responsibility to review the work ahead of time with each subcontractor and to provide written guidance for important issues such as allowable notches and holes. (For tips on planning plumbing lines, see p. 73). Any contracts with subcontractors should include specific stipulations to protect the structure and to assign liability for damages.

Utility Systems

Because the EL structure is preplanned and engineered to such a degree and because it's so difficult to modify after the fact, it's important to go over the plans for the HVAC, plumbing, electrical, and perhaps audio/visual systems prior to construction. This can help prevent unpleasant surprises later. It also can save time and money by eliminating uncertainty for the subs as to where and how different utility systems will be installed.

Holes and Notches

In conventional framing, the allowable notches and holes in structural members are defined by sections of the building code, and a good subcontractor is fully familiar with them. In an EL frame, the allowable holes are defined by specifications from the manufacturer and may vary from project to project. The supplier will provide these specifications, often in the form of a pamphlet attached to the material. However, to clarify the rules and to prevent misunderstandings, it's a good idea to supplement this with a prominent poster or notice.

Poster

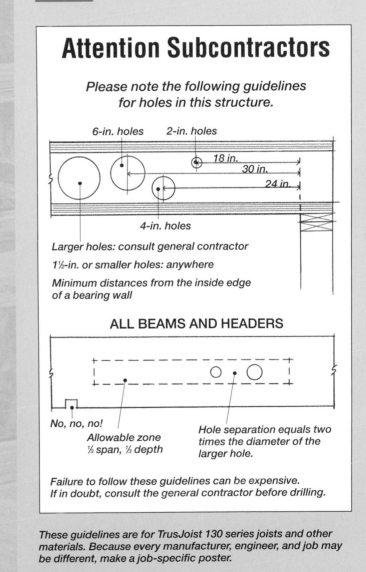

Attention Subcontractors

Please note the following guidelines for holes in this structure.

6-in. holes   2-in. holes

18 in.
30 in.
24 in.

4-in. holes

Larger holes: consult general contractor

1½-in. or smaller holes: anywhere

Minimum distances from the inside edge of a bearing wall

ALL BEAMS AND HEADERS

No, no, no!
Allowable zone
⅓ span, ⅓ depth

Hole separation equals two times the diameter of the larger hole.

Failure to follow these guidelines can be expensive.
If in doubt, consult the general contractor before drilling.

These guidelines are for TrusJoist 130 series joists and other materials. Because every manufacturer, engineer, and job may be different, make a job-specific poster.

■ **PRO** TIP

Aside from drilling and notching guidelines, perhaps the best advice you can give your subs is to consider I-joist flanges as sacred as their daughters' virtue. Don't cut, shave, notch, drill, hammer, or otherwise touch them without asking you first.

■ **PRO** TIP

Don't let HVAC subs close up I-joist bays and use them for ducts, the way they often do with sawn-lumber bays. The webs are far from airtight, the prepunched knockouts can fall out, and airflow can cause wood chips to flake off.

Planning and anticipating problems

I prefer to plan and install systems in an order that's inversely proportional to their flexibility. In other words, what's least flexible in layout gets installed first. That usually means that plumbing waste lines are first, followed by HVAC ductwork, then heating pipes, water supplies, and lastly, wiring. Large electrical conduit should be considered early, like plumbing. Of course, an overview on the part of the designer and GC is helpful, and there can be exceptions to the order. For instance, the plumber can be instructed to avoid areas where HVAC trunks need to go, and frame bays can be prepared for things like recessed light housings.

HVAC

The trunks and ducting used for an HVAC system require such large and specific locations that a good designer or architect will incorporate them into the original design, and a good framer will provide for them from the beginning. By allowing larger bays, longer clear spans, and larger holes (usually, in I-joists), EL can help in designing a duct-friendly frame.

Plumbing

The location, pitch, and destinations of soil or waste lines are critical. The GC and plumber need to locate them on the plan and make sure that they will fit. This includes not only the main lines but also the flanges, drains, traps, and branch lines. Many plumbing fixtures have specific requirements for drain layout, so they need to be specified even before the EL engineer begins his design work. Because of the size of the holes they require, many EL components cannot be drilled for them, and alternate approaches need to be worked out. I've seen houses where commercial-type wall-hung toilets were used to solve these problems and others where elaborate decorative coffered ceilings were built. Anyone who has ever finished a timber-framed home will be familiar with these types of problems and solutions.

Electrical

Most electrical wiring and components are small enough and flexible enough to run almost anywhere. The exceptions are fixtures with rough-in housings, such as heaters, fans, speakers, and recessed lights. It may seem inappropriate to modify a structural framing plan to accommodate lighting, but if the architect, interior designer, and client have a specific lighting plan that calls for precise placement of certain recessed lights, such modifications may be necessary.

Modifying the frame

If a utility problem is anticipated, modifications to the framing plan can be made before construction to accommodate whatever is necessary. Because these changes require the approval of the manufacturer's engineer, allow some communication time. Modifications can be as minor as shifting over a joist or two or as major as reorienting all the joists in a room.

Member substitution

This is one of the simplest solutions. For example, if the plumber needs a 3-in.-dia. hole in an LSL in a given location, the engineer may allow a stronger beam to be substituted, which can then be drilled. Another substitution that often works is a double or triple I-joist replacing a solid member; the I-joist web can be drilled or cut with a larger hole. Be sure to have the engineer's documentation on site for these types of changes. Otherwise, the building official will flag them as violations.

Predrilling Joists

One of the opportunities that arises when framing with I-joists is predrilling holes for pipe and duct runs before the joists are installed. By stacking a set of joists on sawhorses or on the floor, a pilot hole can be drilled through the webs, followed by drilled or sawed holes. This saves marking and cutting the holes overhead in the joist bays later. Large neat holes for duct runs can be cut comfortably this way, and the pilot hole can even be drilled at an angle for a sloped pipe run.

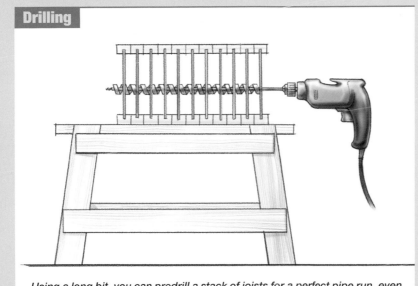

Drilling

Using a long bit, you can predrill a stack of joists for a perfect pipe run, even a sloped one. After the pilot hole is drilled, flip the joists one at a time and use a hole saw. Keep them in order.

Adding a member

This is a field correction that can often be made without engineering approval and that most building officials will approve. For example, an I-joist flange that needs to be notched for a shower drain can be sistered with an added joist alongside. This is generally a straightforward fix.

Fixing a problem

Occasionally, despite the best intentions of everyone concerned, a problem arises that requires repair. EL manufacturers all provide assistance with these situations. I've found that a phone call to the engi- neer, followed up with a sketch on the plan and perhaps some digital photos will usually result in a field correction specification. Sometimes this is as simple as a stamped letter certifying that the structure is OK as built. More often, some form of reinforcement is specified, rang- ing from added hardware or gusset plates to additional framing members. The worst-case scenario involves removal, redesign, and reconstruction of the prob- lem area. In any case, the solution will be provided and certified reasonably quickly.

Here's an example of clean, neat wiring, with a hole drilled where it is needed and good stapling. However, be aware that the staple points will come through the other side of the web.

Other Subcontracting Issues

A number of other issues may arise when subcontractors encounter engineered lumber. It is impossible to anticipate everything, but here are some of the most common problems and solutions.

Fastening

Stapling cable and wires to the webs of I-joists is troublesome because the webs are hard and bouncy, so subcontractors tend to avoid doing it. Make sure that they use enough staples to meet code and that they're aware that the points of their staples will poke out the other side of the webs, potentially damaging wires or pipes. They also like to staple along the flanges instead; this is OK so long as they keep the wires out of reach of flooring nails and drywall screws.

Hello, Houston, we've got a problem down here...

Nailing Off

In some areas, nailing off roof sheathing is a subcontracted trade. Nailing subs like I-joist rafters because they're flat, wide, and hard to miss. A worthwhile caution, however: Avoid nailing in straight lines right down the middle of I-joists. Doing so can weaken the web-to-flange attachment.

Nailing

Staggering nails in subflooring or sheathing from side to side is a good idea. A few in the middle won't hurt, but a perfect row of nails, such as with a chalkline, is a bad idea.

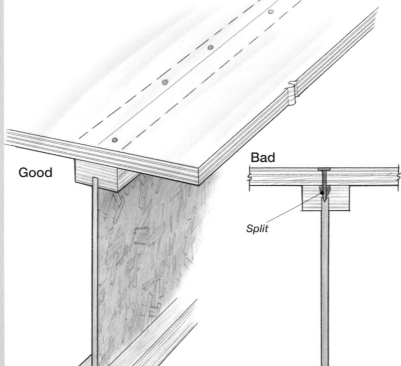

Good

Bad

Split

Blocks to Support Pipes

Short blocks of 2x material that fit between the webs and rest on the I-joist flanges are an easy and popular way to secure pipes and ducts. Precut a pile of them while doing the wall framing.

A pile of these blocks will save your subs time. They fit between the webs, rest on the flanges, and are easily secured in position with screws or nails.

Bay sizes

Many of the housings used by sub trades, such as boxes for heaters, fans, fan coil units, lights, recessed plumbing fixtures, stereo and audio components, and other built-in items, are designed for standard joist and stud bays. Sawn lumber at 16 in. o.c. leaves a 14½-in. bay; I-joists at 16 in. o.c. can leave as little as 12½ in. This is often a problem in floors and ceilings. Try to anticipate this issue, and do not allow subs to shave the edges of flanges to get the required bay width.

Knockouts

Many I-joists come with prepunched holes in the webs, which can be knocked out using a hammer. My experience has been that these holes are almost never located or sized appropriately for neat

professional utility runs, and they don't always break out cleanly. Subcontractors using these holes often acquire the unfortunate habit of making additional holes with their hammer claws instead of a drill or saw. This leads to messy and unprofessional work.

Temporary loading

Many sub trades use large quantities of heavy materials. These include drywall, tile, backer board, bagged products, masonry, flooring, siding, roofing, and decking. Once, I was surprised to find three 55-gallon drums full of water in the middle of a living room floor. It is critical that these heavy loads not be stacked in concentrated locations on EL floor or roof systems. EL components, especially I-joists, do not have the natural resiliency of sawn lumber and can acquire permanent deflections from relatively short-term overloading.

Staging (also called scaffolding) is another potential loading problem. A mason's stand of pipe staging, for instance, can concentrate heavy loads on just two floor joists, leading to excessive deflection or even failure.

There are several ways to deal with the issue of temporary loading, besides simply forbidding it. Identify areas in the structure where the loads will be adequately supported from below. Use staging planks to spread out loads over larger sections of framing. If necessary, you can insert temporary supports under floors that might be susceptible to overload damage.

Fire protection

Fire-suppression systems, or sprinkler systems, are treated the same way as other pipe runs, but their locations are usually precisely engineered and should be reviewed and prioritized early in the subcontracting process. Alarm systems, on

Insulation

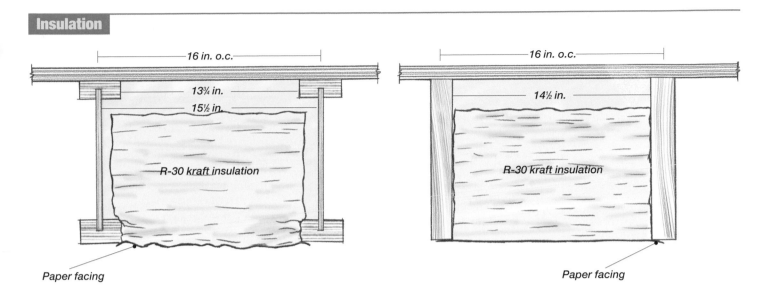

Paper facing

Paper facing

Conventional framing has 14½-in. joist bays, so standard insulation is designed to fit just right. I-joists have less width between the flanges and more between the webs. This causes the paper facing to wrinkle and potentially leaves an airspace along the webs.

Fire Protection

Some codes and building officials are beginning to consider I-joists as a liability in structure fires, similar to floor and roof trusses. The issue is complicated, but essentially I-joists can fail quickly and catastrophically during a fire, as the lower flanges burn through. This can lead to sudden unexpected collapse, endangering fire-fighters and occupants.

Because of these concerns, extra fireproofing may be required. Codes also may call for more extensive and expensive fire alarm and suppression equipment, insurance requirements, and possibly mandatory labeling on the building exterior.

the other hand, are very flexible and can be installed last.

Insulation

Because the webs of I-joists are typically ½ in. thick, as opposed to the 1½-in. thickness of dimension lumber, standard fiberglass insulation does not completely fill the bays. This is generally an issue only in roof construction, since most floors get only zone or sound insulation. There

are several options here. One is to add insulation along the webs. Another is to accept the lower R-value of trapped air, which, with careful installation, will be slight. The last is to use an alternative insulation, such as a blown-in product. At this time, specifically sized insulation is not available for I-joists, but this may well change as EL construction becomes more common.

Index

A

AdvanTech Subflooring, 17
Alarm systems, 118–19
APA (American Plywood
    Association). See
    Engineered Wood
    Association
Architectural glulams, 57
Aspenite. See Flakeboard
Attic trusses, 107

B

Bar trusses, 16, 108, 109
Beam pockets, 61, 62
Beams, 56–69
    assembling, 64–68
    connectors/hangers for,
        20–24, 31
    definition of, 9, 11
    flush, 67
    flush vs. dropped, 58–59, 60
    glulam, 5, 10, 12, 13, 57, 65
    installation of, 69
    LSL, 65
    LVL, 58, 64–68, 94
    PSL, 58, 65
    ridge, 91, 92, 93, 94
    spliced, 66, 67
    steel, 68
    supports for, 60–63
    types of, 11–15, 57
Bearing length, 60–61
Bearing plates, 21, 22, 89
Blocking panels, 73, 78–81
Building codes, 6, 33, 113

C

Cantilevers, 78
Carrying beams. See Beams
CDX plywood, 16
Circular saw, 49–50
Columns
    for beams and girders, 60, 61
    definition of, 9, 11
    LSL, 89
    PSL, 89
    in walls, 87–88
Compressive strength, 9, 18–19
Construction techniques
    conventional vs. EL, 32–35
    hybrid, 16, 40–41, 94
Cutting, 44, 52–54

D

Design
    for engineered lumber,
        32–35, 39–40
    floor, 70–73
    modifications to, 114–15
    roof, 90–95
    software for, 71–73, 90
Dimensional lumber
    characteristics of, 11
    defects in, 10
    headers, 85, 87
    in hybrid construction,
        40–41
    treated, 27
Dormers, 92
Dropped beams, 58–59, 60
Ducts, 114, 118

E

Electrical systems, 113–14, 116
Engineered lumber (EL)
    benefits of, 6–7
    characteristics of, 11
    vs. conventional construc-
        tion, 32–35
    costs of, 36, 38
    design for, 32–35, 39–40
    disposal of, 45
    future of, 19
    handling, 45–49
    history of, 5
    holes and notches in, 113
    in hybrid construction,
        40–41
    manufactures of, 5, 6
    moisture and, 15, 49
    order and delivery, 46–47
    safety for, 42–45
    selling, 34
    spacing for, 39, 40
    storage of, 46
    techniques for, 36, 37, 52–54
    types of, 8–17
    unloading, 46–47
Engineered Wood Association,
    5, 6
Engineering, 33, 35

F

Finger-jointed studs, 84–85
Fire protection, 118, 119
Fitch beams, 68
Flakeboard, 17
Flanges, 15–16, 24, 114
Floors, 70–81
    blocking panels for, 78–81
    conventional vs. EL, 40
    designing, 70–73
    framing sequence for, 74
    hybrid, 41
    I-joists for, 74–78
    layout, 73–74
    openings in, 74
    rim joists for, 77, 80–81
    squash blocks for, 80
    squeaking, 78
    subflooring, 17, 25, 81
    trusses for, 108, 109
Flush beams, 58–59, 60
Footings, 40, 61
Foundations, 40, 61, 62

G

Gable roof, 91, 94, 95, 107, 110
Girders, 11, 20–24, 31, 56–69
Glulams
    architectural, 57
    beams, 65
    crown of, 10
    description of, 5, 12, 13
Gunpowder-actuated tools, 69

H

Hammer, framing, 50, 52
Hanger nails, 19, 51
Hangers, 21–24
    custom, 26
    heavy-duty, 23–24
    hip and valley, 26–27, 100
    I-joist, 22–23, 31

installation of, 31, 45
    load capacity of, 73
    rafter, 25, 26–27, 93, 99, 100
    removing, 30
    roof, 25–27, 93–94
Hardware, 18–31
    conventional vs. EL, 35
    roof, 90–91, 93–94,
        104–105
    See also Hangers; Steel
        connectors
HCP (Hip corner plates), 26–27
Headers
    definition of, 11
    dimensional lumber, 85, 87
    hangers for, 25
    I-joist, 85–86, 87
    LSL, 86, 87
    LVL, 86–87
    PSL, 87
    roof, 92, 99–100
    wall, 85–87
HGUS hangers, 26
Hip roof, 26–27, 92, 100, 103,
    111
HRC (Hip ridge connectors),
    26–27
HVAC systems, 113–14, 118
Hybrid systems, 16, 40–41, 94

I

I-beams, steel, 68
I-joists
    blocking panels, 73
    boxing in, 118
    cutting and nailing, 44,
        52–53
    defects in, 10
    description of, 15–16, 17
    development of, 5
    fire protection for, 119
    flanges, 15–16, 24, 114
    floor, 73–78
    handling, 47–49
    hangers for, 22–23, 30, 31
    headers from, 85–86, 87
    for hips and valleys, 92,
        100, 103
    hybrid bar/I-joist, 16
    jigs for, 55
    knockouts in, 118
    moisture and, 15, 49
    nailing, 45
    predrilling, 115
    rafters, 96–99, 103
    roof, 90
    safety for, 43
    spacing for, 39, 40, 74
    standardization of, 16
    web stiffeners for, 97, 99
Insulation, 119
ITT hangers, 22–23
IUT hangers, 22–23

J

Jack rafters, 100, 101, 102
Jigs, 55
Joists
    definition of, 11
    hangers for, 21–24, 31
    rim, 54, 77, 80–81
    See also I-joists

L

Lally column caps (LCCs), 20, 21, 63
Lally columns, 22, 40, 60
Laminated beams, glued. See Glulams
Level plans, 34
Loads, 9, 38, 39–40, 118
LSL (Laminated strand lumber)
    beams, 65
    columns, 87–88, 89
    cutting and nailing, 54
    description of, 12, 14
    development of, 5
    headers, 86, 87
    rafters, 96
    studs and plates, 82–84
LSSUI rafter hanger, 25, 93
LSTA strap, 28, 29
Lumber. See Dimensional lumber; Engineered lumber
LVL (Laminated veneer lumber)
    beams, 58, 64–68, 94
    cutting and nailing, 52–53
    description of, 12, 14–15
    headers, 86–87
    marking on, 50
    rafters, 26, 96
    ridge beams, 94
    safety for, 44, 45

M

Marking/measuring tools, 50
Moisture, 15, 49

N

Nailing, 45, 50–52, 117
Nails, 19, 51

O

OSB (Oriented strand board), 16–17, 85, 88–89, 97

P

Parallel chord trusses, 109
Plates
    LSL, 82–84
    steel bearing, 21, 22, 89
Plot plans, 72, 91, 94
Plumbing, 73, 113–14, 118
Plywood, 16, 85
Pneumatic nailers, 45, 51, 52
Pocket framer's reference, 36, 37
Pockets, beam, 61, 62
PSL (Parallel strand lumber)
    beams, 58, 65
    columns, 87, 88, 89
    cutting and nailing, 54
    description of, 12, 13
    development of, 5
    headers, 87
    marking on, 50
    rafters, 96

R

Rafters
    hangers for, 25, 26–27, 93, 99, 100
    I-joist, 96–99, 103
    jack, 100, 101, 102
    jigs for, 55

    pattern, 94
    spacing for, 39–40
    structural, 96
    tensile connectors for, 28–29, 31
    ties for, 104, 105
    types of, 96
Renovations, 41
Ridge beams, 91, 92, 93, 94
Ridge connectors, 26–27, 28, 29, 31
Rim joists, 54, 77, 80–81
Ring-shank nails, 51
Roofs, 90–105
    conventional vs. EL, 35
    designing, 90–95
    gable, 91, 94, 95, 107, 110
    hardware for, 25, 26–27, 93–94
    headers and holes, 92, 99–100
    hips and valleys, 26–27, 92, 100, 103, 111
    hybrid, 41, 94
    overhangs and blocking, 102–103
    ridge beams, 91, 92, 93, 94
    sheathing, 102, 105, 117
    steel connectors for, 25–27
    trusses for, 106–11
    web stiffeners for, 97, 99
    See also Rafters

S

Safety, 42–45
Sawdust, 44
Saws, 49–50
Scissor trusses, 107
Sections, 9
Sheathing, 29, 88–89, 102, 105, 117
Sheet goods, 16–17
Simpson Strong-Tie Company, 19–29
Software, design, 71–73, 90
Spikes, 51
Square (Tool), 50
Squash blocks, 80, 89
Stacking, 46
Staples, 116
Steel beams, 68
Steel bearing plates, 21, 22, 89
Steel connectors, 19–31
    for beams and girders, 20–24, 31
    custom, 31
    for roofs, 25–27
    tensile connectors, 27–31
Stick nailer, 51
Storage, 46
Strap ties, ridge, 27, 28, 31
Strength, 9, 18–19, 89
Studs, 82–85
Subcontractors, 112–19
Subfascia, 102, 103
Subflooring, 17, 25, 81

T

Tape measure, 50
Tensile connectors, 27–31
Tensile strength, 9, 18–19

Toenails, 78
Tools, 44, 49–52
Transportation, 46–47
Treated lumber, 27
TrusJoist, 5
Trusses, 16, 106–11

U

United Steel Products, 29, 31
Unloading, 46–47
Utility systems, 113–14, 116, 118

V

Valleys, 26–27, 92, 100, 103
Variable pitch rafter connectors, 27
Vertical load, 38, 39–40

W

W-series hangers, 24
Walls, 82–89
    columns in, 87–88
    design of, 39
    headers for, 85–87
    hybrid, 41
    OSB sheathing for, 88–89
    studs for, 82–85
    tensile connectors for, 28
    zone framing for, 38, 84
Warranty, 33
Web stiffeners, 15, 97, 99
Wind-resistance, 38
Wood, solid. See Dimensional lumber

Z

Zone framing, 38, 84

Taunton's FOR PROS BY PROS Series
A collection of the best articles from *Fine Homebuilding* magazine.

Other Books in the Series:

Taunton's For Pros By Pros:
RENOVATING A BATHROOM

ISBN 1-56158-584-X
Product #070702
$17.95 U.S.
$25.95 Canada

Taunton's For Pros By Pros:
BUILDING ADDITIONS

ISBN 1-56158-699-4
Product #070779
$17.95 U.S.
$25.95 Canada

Taunton's For Pros By Pros:
BUILDING STAIRS

ISBN 1-56158-653-6
Product #070742
$17.95 U.S.
$25.95 Canada

Taunton's For Pros By Pros:
BUILT-INS AND STORAGE

ISBN 1-56158-700-1
Product #070780
$17.95 U.S.
$25.95 Canada

Taunton's For Pros By Pros:
EXTERIOR SIDING,
TRIM & FINISHES

ISBN 1-56158-652-8
Product #070741
$17.95 U.S.
$25.95 Canada

Taunton's For Pros By Pros:
FINISH CARPENTRY

ISBN 1-56158-536-X
Product #070633
$17.95 U.S.
$25.95 Canada

Taunton's For Pros By Pros:
FOUNDATIONS AND
CONCRETE WORK

ISBN 1-56158-537-8
Product #070635
$17.95 U.S.
$25.95 Canada

Taunton's For Pros By Pros:
RENOVATING A KITCHEN

ISBN 1-56158-540-8
Product #070637
$17.95 U.S.
$25.95 Canada

Taunton's For Pros By Pros:
FRAMING ROOFS

ISBN 1-56158-538-6
Product #070634
$17.95 U.S.
$25.95 Canada

Taunton's For Pros By Pros:
BUILDING PORCHES AND
DECKS

ISBN 1-56158-539-4
Product #070636
$17.95 U.S.
$25.95 Canada

Taunton's For Pros By Pros:
BUILDING TIPS AND
TECHNIQUES

ISBN 1-56158-687-0
Product #070766
$17.95 U.S.
$25.95 Canada

Taunton's For Pros By Pros:
ATTICS, DORMERS, AND
SKYLIGHTS

ISBN 1-56158-779-6
Product #070834
$17.95 U.S.
$25.95 Canada

Taunton's For Pros By Pros:
FRAMING FLOORS, WALLS,
AND CEILINGS

ISBN 1-56158-758-3
Product #070821
$17.95 U.S.
$25.95 Canada

Taunton's For Pros By Pros:
ROOFING, FLASHING &
WATERPROOFING

ISBN 1-56158-778-8
Product #070833
$17.95 U.S.
$25.95 Canada

Taunton's For Pros By Pros:
TILING PLANNING, LAYOUT,
AND INSTALLATION

ISBN 1-56158-788-5
Product #070843
$17.95 U.S.
$25.95 Canada

For more information
visit our website at
www.taunton.com.